Activities

FOR STRIKING A BALANCE IN

Early Literacy

NANCY LEE CECIL

California State University, Sacramento

HOLCOMB HATHAWAY, PUBLISHERS

Scottsdale, Arizona

Library of Congress Cataloging-in-Publication Data

Cecil, Nancy Lee.
    Activities for striking a balance in early literacy / Nancy Lee Cecil.
        p.   cm.
    Includes bibliographical references.
    ISBN 1-890871-31-1
        1. Language arts (Early childhood)—United States.   2. Early childhood
education—Activity programs—United States.   I. Title.

LB1139.5.L35 C43 2001
372.6—dc21

                                                                00-056743

 Holcomb Hathaway, Publishers, Inc.
        6207 North Cattle Track Road
        Scottsdale, Arizona 85250
(480) 991-7881
www.hh-pub.com

10 9 8 7 6 5 4 3

ISBN 1-890871-31-1

Printed in the United States of America.

BRIEF CONTENTS

For the complete Contents, see page iv.

CONTENTS

Activities to Develop Phonemic Awareness   29

Activities for Phonics Instruction   57

Activities for Spelling through Experimenting with Print   85

Activities to Increase Vocabulary   113

6 Activities to Foster Reading Comprehension 141

7 Activities to Inspire Young Writers 169

Appendices

PREFACE

The goal of *Activities for Striking a Balance in Early Literacy* is to provide teacher-tested instructional strategies, coupled with effective reflection activities, to preservice and inservice teachers of literacy. This goal underscores the premise that the teacher is an educational leader and decision-maker in the classroom who influences how literacy instruction will be presented and who ultimately affects the students' enjoyment of reading.

In this book, which complements the more theoretical *Striking a Balance: Positive practices for Early Literacy* (Holcomb Hathaway, Publishers, 1999), I offer a broad spectrum of methodologies, techniques, and approaches for literacy instruction that have been found to be highly effective in today's diverse classrooms. I hope that prospective teachers will find this book valuable as a basis for identifying sound educational practices and as a guide for making systematic, logical, and humane instructional choices about literacy both in their teacher-training placements and, later, in their own classrooms. Although *Activities* is intended primarily for literacy courses for preservice and inservice teachers, it may be used as a reference book for a variety of other purposes as well. For example, students in tutoring classes who have not yet decided to become teachers will find in the activities and reflection questions valuable guidance for preparing effective literacy lessons for individual children. Seasoned teachers will find the book helpful as a "refresher," or as a source of interesting new activities to bring to their classrooms. The activities also are ideal for preservice courses using a reflective teaching approach. The teachers in training try out activities on each other and then analyze the results of their teaching effectiveness through the reflection questions presented in this book.

The activities have been chosen specifically according to three discrete criteria:

1. They are designed expressly for, or are adaptable to, English language learners (ELL) and therefore have the prerequisite sheltering necessary for this diverse population.

2. They are highly motivational activities that will complement the more structured nature of currently-in-use literacy materials.

3. They incorporate state-of-the-art understanding of the best practices for teaching young children to become literate human beings.

Each activity offers the reader a suggested grade level, although this may be adjusted according to the achievement level of the group of students in question. Each activity also includes the materials needed for the activity, carefully delineated step-by-step instructions, the educational purposes for selecting the activity, and how the the teacher can evaluate the effectiveness of each activity. Reflection questions at the end of each section may be used to determine the teacher's effectiveness, to ascertain changes that should be made in subsequent implementation of the activities, and to examine insights the teacher might have gained about the topic of instruction.

Throughout *Activities,* I have made reference to materials or discussions that can be found in my textbook, *Striking a Balance.* These references (in the format "SAB, p. xx") are for your information only and need be pursued only if you wish to do so. (The textbook is also available from Holcomb Hathaway, Publishers.)

ACKNOWLEDGMENTS

Reviewers of the manuscript provided critical feedback that I welcomed and incorporated into the final product. Classroom teachers field-tested the activities and offered many ideas about clarity, scope, and additions. I extend heartfelt thanks to them for their invaluable guidance: Betty Dean Newman, Athens State University; Laurie Williams, University of Pittsburgh; Catherine Kurkjian, Central Connecticut State University; Clara Carroll, Harding University; Diane Barone, University of Nevada, Reno; and Sherron Killingsworth Roberts, University of Central Florida.

I also would like to thank Linda Toren, California State University, Stanislaus, who used a draft of the manuscript in her professional development seminar. We wish to thank the following teachers for providing feedback about the activities from the perspective of the classroom teacher: Marjorie Borgquist, Sousbyville, CA; Rita R. Millsaps, Mokelumne Hill Elementary; Heather L. Holland, Jenny Lind Elementary; Kathleen Davey, Avery Middle School; Gretchen Johnson, Plymouth Elementary School; Mary Gylide, Sonora Elementary School; A. Zgraggen, Jameston Elementary School; Liz Miller, Curtis Creek School District; Sandy Fisher, Curtis Creek School District; and Gennalee Young, Cooperopolis Elementary School.

The support of my publisher has been helpful beyond words. Colette Kelly, acquisitions editor, worked day and night to bring this book to fruition. She continues to share my vision of a literacy program that is balanced, creating readers who can read and who want to read.

Finally, I again extend my eternal gratitude to my husband, Gary, and daughter, Chrissy, who were infinitely patient as I took time away from coffee chats and other family activities to think about, write, and edit this book. Your feedback and interest in what I do is astounding—even when all of life appears to revolve around my writing.

1

ACTIVITIES TO DEVELOP EARLY LITERACY

Introduction

Emergent literacy is said to begin the moment a child enters this world. In fact, some reading experts say that literacy learning occurs at a certain level even while the child is still in the womb! Early in life, as children hear sounds, utter their first words, ask questions, listen to stories and conversations, and pretend to read and write, they are deeply involved in the process of becoming literate.

To help children become ready for more formalized instruction in the basics of reading and writing, teachers and parents can do much to ensure later success. By helping children to become fluent speakers and by encouraging them to become familiar with how print works—whether by calling attention to the sounds of words, their shapes, or the way words are put on a page of text—we are encouraging children in their ability to acquire a good foundation for future literacy.

The activities in this section are expressly designed to foster the process of literacy acquisition for the very young child in a preschool or kindergarten setting. The activities are appropriate for most preliterate children. Some are designed especially for the needs of children who are grappling with the English language and are busy acquiring a receptive and speaking vocabulary in English—English language learners (ELL). Other activities may be more appropriate for children who already have received a wide variety of experiences in conversation, listening to sounds, and book handling—such children may benefit from the greater challenge that these activities offer. The detailed activities are followed by some brief, practical classroom suggestions and selected references to children's literature for further reading about this special stage of development.

Draw a Story

SUGGESTED GRADE LEVEL *PreK–K*

PURPOSE Through drawing as a precursor to writing, children can respond to literature, develop story ideas, reflect on what they know about a topic, and demonstrate their understanding of story structure. In this activity, preliterate children can draw instead of write to compose their ideas.

MATERIALS
- Paper folded into quarters
- Pencils
- Inspirational object (optional)

PROCEDURE

1. With the children, brainstorm some interesting ideas they have about their lives, their families, their toys, their friends, or topics from books that have been read to them or television programs they have seen. Optionally, show the children an interesting object and allow them to describe it. On the chalkboard, write a word or several words for each of these ideas, sounding them out for the children.

2. Give each child a large piece of construction paper folded into quarters. Ask the children to choose one of the ideas that have been discussed, or any others that occur to them, and draw pictures to show how they feel about the topic they have chosen. Ask them to draw the pictures in the four boxes in order (demonstrate this idea by modeling your own four pictures; show children through thinking aloud why you are choosing this order).

3. Go around to each of the children, asking them to tell about their pictures. Above or below each picture, write a caption containing a key concept or an important word from what the child tells you, saying the word aloud slowly and segmenting the letters (sounding out the

word) in front of the child. Review the words with each child by saying them along with the child.

4. Have the children share their drawings in small groups, and then have one child from each group tell about the group's drawings to the whole class.

ASSESSMENT   Take anecdotal notes on how each child was able to follow directions and draw four pictures corresponding to people and other important things in his or her life. Informally, see whether each child is able to show you where a word begins and ends.

Notes for next time . . .

_____

_____

_____

_____

_____

_____

_____

_____

_____

_____

_____

_____

_____

Treasure Hunt

ACTIVITIES TO DEVELOP EARLY LITERACY

SUGGESTED
GRADE LEVEL   *PreK–K*

PURPOSE   Children's success in decoding depends largely on a basic understanding of how written print works. This gamelike activity will help children become familiar with the parts of a book and how print is arranged in text, or "concepts about print."

MATERIALS
- A Big Book of an unfamiliar story
- The same story in small texts, enough for every other child in the group
- A pointer

PROCEDURE

1. Have a small group of children sit in a semi-circle on the floor. Sit facing the children in a chair so all can clearly see the Big Book.

2. Before reading the story aloud, point out to the children the author's and illustrator's names and the dedication. Explain each of these features. Then, during the reading, call the children's attention to the following concepts of print:

   - The beginning of the book
   - A word
   - A letter
   - The first word on a page
   - The last word on a page
   - Punctuation
   - An illustration

Continued.

3. After reading the story to the children, explain that you are going to ask them to go on a special "treasure hunt," searching for different things that can be found in a book.

4. Pair the children.

5. Beginning with the author, the illustrator, and so forth, ask each pair of children to find one book feature at a time. When each pair has located the feature requested, invite one child to come up and, using the pointer, indicate that same feature in the Big Book. Let the other child in each pair tell how they discovered the feature asked for.

6. Use the same procedure for *all* the concepts of print listed. Make this treasure hunt a part of your regular read-a-loud routine until all the children are familiar with all of the book-related features.

ASSESSMENT   Using the corresponding small books, go around to each child and ask whether each can find the items discussed in this lesson. Use a checklist for each item, or use the Concepts about Print Assessment (included in the textbook, *Striking a Balance [SAB]*, p. 268). Place the checklist in each child's file.

Notes for next time . . .

_____

_____

_____

_____

_____

_____

_____

_____

Words in the World

SUGGESTED GRADE LEVEL   *K–1*

PURPOSE   By having children talk about the words with which they are familiar, they begin to grasp the concept that print carries a message and represents concepts they know.

MATERIALS
- Chart paper
- Markers
- Stop sign made from red construction paper
- Labels for common objects in the room (desk, table, door, closet, computer, etc.)
- Masking tape

PROCEDURE

1. Hold up the stop sign for the children to see. Tell them this is a sign they see almost every day when they are in the car with their family. It contains a message for drivers telling them what they must do. Ask if anyone knows what the sign says.

2. Say the word "stop" with the children as you point to the letters in sequence.

3. Ask the children if they can think of any other signs they know about and can recognize. As they mention signs, such as K-Mart, McDonald's, or Chevrolet, for example, write these words on the board, asking the children to contribute any letters they know. Later place these words on a Word Wall.

4. Tell the children they now are going to put signs on the things they use every day in the classroom.

5. With each label, read the word to the children while pointing to each letter slowly. Ask for a volunteer to tape the label on the appropriate classroom item.

ASSESSMENT   Make a list of all the signs and labels in the room. Have each child "read" the signs and labels as you check off the ones each child is able to read. Additionally, if a child is unable to say a word by sight, indicate if he or she is able to recognize any of the letters or sounds.

Notes for next time . . .

_____

_____

_____

_____

_____

_____

_____

_____

_____

_____

_____

_____

_____

_____

_____

_____

Nursery Rhymes

**SUGGESTED
GRADE LEVEL** *K–1*

PURPOSE

Young children enjoy the joyful rhymes, rhythm, and repetition of nursery rhymes. Rhymes can be simply read to the children, or they can be chanted chorally, used to inspire creative drama, or serve as the basis for composing unique language experience stories.

MATERIALS

- Nursery rhyme anthology book(s), such as Mother Goose
- Language experience chart and paper
- Triangles or wooden sticks (optional)

PROCEDURE

1. Read aloud a nursery rhyme, such as Jack and Jill, several times for the children. Invite them to chime in as they feel comfortable saying it with you.

2. Introduce the children to some choral speaking experiences. Because most nursery rhymes are easily memorized, the children do not have to be able to read. Practice different choral arrangements, such as the boys speaking every other line; or soloists speaking certain lines and the others becoming the chorus who speak the remaining lines. Have the children recite the rhyme in a whisper but say the rhyming words loudly, or recite the rhyme in a loud voice but whisper the rhyming words. Also, rudimentary instruments, such as triangles or wooden sticks, can be used to keep time to the rhythm, or meter.

3. Use nursery rhymes to help the children identify the parts of a verse—beginning, middle, and ending—such as in Jack and Jill:

   > Jack and Jill went up the hill to get a pail of water. (beginning)
   > Jack fell down and broke his crown. (middle)
   > And Jill came tumbling after. (end)

   Ask the children to identify the first event in the rhyme, the second event, and the last event.

4. Divide the class into pairs and have them act out what happened in the beginning of the verse, the middle of the verse, and the end of the verse. Encourage the children to extend their parts by adding dialogue to accompany each event. Allow each group an opportunity to act out its interpretation of the rhyme for the rest of the group.

5. After reading each nursery rhyme, write a story about it using the Language Experience Approach format. For example, after reading Jack and Jill, ask the children: What do you think

4 *Nursery Rhymes*

Continued.

Jack got a bump on his head when he fell down the hill. Jill helped him up. Their mom was angry because they got dirty. They did it again the next day but they didn't fall down.

happened after Jack and Jill fell down the hill? Were they hurt? Did they ever climb the hill again? Did they ever get the water they were after? Transcribe the children's answers to these questions to create a novel Language Experience Story.

6. Provide copies of the Language Experience Story for each child in the class. Place the story on the top of the paper and leave plenty of space at the bottom for the children to create illustrations to accompany their cooperatively composed story.

ASSESSMENT Ask individual children to retell the story in their own words. Select certain words at random and ask them to find the words in the story. Finally, ask them to point to the following concepts of print: a word, a letter, the beginning of a sentence, and the end of a sentence.

Oral Vocabulary Builder

ACTIVITIES TO DEVELOP EARLY LITERACY

SUGGESTED GRADE LEVEL *PreK–3*

PURPOSE

A young child learns most words from hearing them spoken in conversation or through media, or having heard them being read in the context of a story. If children have a limited English vocabulary, they need much practice in oral language, both through listening and by attempting to generate thoughts in English. This activity provides practice for English language learners (ELL) and also offers a challenging opportunity for native English speakers to think about selecting appropriate words in a sentence.

MATERIALS

- Simple phrase cards or phrases written on the chalkboard
- Paper and crayons for each child

PROCEDURE

1. On the chalkboard each day, write a phrase containing a simple subject and predicate familiar to native English speakers but possibly new vocabulary to English language learners. Hand out cards containing the same phrase to each child. Examples:

    Baby cries.

    Boy ran.

    Dog sat.

    Bird sang.

    Door closed.

The baby girl cried when she saw the tiger growl.

2. Read the phrase aloud to the children as they point to each word and say it after you. Repeat this step several times until each child can say the phrase accurately.

3. Give the children crayons and two sheets of paper each, and have them draw a picture depicting the action in the phrase. Invite the children to share their drawings.

4. Explain to the children: The words I gave you don't tell us much about the baby and why she is crying. Can someone add a word or words to the phrase that will tell us what the baby

looks like or why she is crying? (If the children have trouble getting started, offer examples, such as: The little baby is crying because she got stung by a bumblebee.) After allowing children a few minutes to think, go around the room soliciting new sentences from the children that add words, phrases, and clauses to the original phrase.

5. Ask the children to use their second sheet of paper to create a new drawing that incorporates some new descriptions of why the baby might be crying, what he or she looks like, and any other new information that emerged from the new sentences.

6. As the children are drawing, go around the room and ask each child to tell you what new sentence they are illustrating. Transcribe the revised sentence for them underneath their pictures. Encourage the children to share their revised drawings. Discuss which drawing they like better and why.

ASSESSMENT   Assess each child's ability to tell you the exact sentence he or she is drawing. On subsequent occasions with this activity, note increases in the number of words (e.g., adjectives, adverbs, and clauses) the child uses to elaborate on the sentence.

Notes for next time . . .

_____

_____

_____

_____

_____

_____

_____

_____

The Alphabet in Five Senses 6

SUGGESTED GRADE LEVEL *K–1*

PURPOSE Because the basic elements of all reading and writing are the letters of the alphabet, being familiar with these letters is crucial to becoming literate. Using all five senses instead of simply the child's auditory and visual senses makes learning accessible to all kinds of learners, especially those for whom English is a second language.

MATERIALS
- Overhead transparency of the alphabet in lower-case letters
- Sandpaper cards, one for each letter of the alphabet
- Scissors
- A quart of fine sand or salt
- Canned whipped cream
- Waxed paper

PROCEDURE

1. Teach the children the alphabet song (for some children, this may be a review). Then ask the children to sing the song slowly as you point out the letters on the overhead transparency. Sing the song slowly a third time, inviting individual children to come up and point out the letters on the transparency as they are sung.

2. Present a new letter each day, calling the children's attention to its characteristic shape and any ascending or descending features. Have the children look at the letter carefully and then draw the letter in the air with their imaginary "sky pencils."

3. From the sandpaper, cut out each of the letters and hand them out to the children as you introduce each letter. Have individual children touch the outline of the letter on the sandpaper, feeling the rough shape of the letter as they say aloud the name of the letter.

4. Place a thin layer of salt or fine sand in a shoebox lid or other container and have the children, one at a time, trace the letters in the sand or salt as they say the letters aloud and hear the teacher and classmates say them.

5. Finally, tape a piece of waxed paper to each child's desk. Squirt a small amount of whipped cream onto the waxed paper on the children's desks. (Make sure the children's hands are clean for this activity!) As you call out the letters, invite the children to trace the letters in the whipped cream. As you go around the room and check the letters, invite the children to smell and taste their letter. When they have done this, offer an alliterative phrase for them to announce: For example: Y (or whatever letter has been introduced) tastes yummy! or E is excellent! or T is tasty! This is a way for children to eventually associate sounds with letters.

6. Use the above multisensory method to introduce and reinforce all the letters of the alphabet in an enjoyable way.

ASSESSMENT   Follow the lesson with an individual assessment of letter names and sounds. To do this, write the names of all the letters in large block letters, lower case, leaving room for a checkmark beside each letter. Run off enough copies for each student. Ask each child to tell you the name of the letter and its sound. Alternatively, use the Knowledge of Sounds and Letters Checklist (*SAB,* p. 280).

Notes for next time . . .

_____

_____

_____

_____

_____

_____

_____

_____

_____

Who Is It?

**SUGGESTED
GRADE LEVEL** *PreK–K*

PURPOSE   The main objective of this activity is to have the children recognize that language is made up of many different sounds. Also as a result of this activity, the children will better understand the importance of our sense of hearing and the value of listening carefully to another person. In this case, they will be focusing not only on words that are spoken but also on the intonation, inflection, dialect or accent, pitch, and volume of a voice. The children will struggle to think of appropriate vocabulary words to describe differences in voices. This activity helps children to consider what goes into the recognition of a familiar voice. They also begin to understand how we usually rely on the sense of sight and the sense of hearing at the same time.

MATERIALS
- Tape recorder
- Audiotape

PROCEDURE

1. In advance of the lesson, tape-record every child in the room individually saying the same sentence, such as: We are having pizza for lunch today! Write this sentence on the chalkboard and say it with the children chorally.

2. Have the children sit at their desks with their eyes closed (so they do not pick up visual cues from the face of the person with the mystery voice). Play the recording of the first child saying the sentence. Ask the children to guess whose voice they think it is. Write the names of the guesses on the chalkboard. Finally, reveal the mystery voice.

3. After each mystery voice has been revealed, invite the children to discuss the answers to the following questions:

How did you guess who owned the mystery voice?

Could you tell if the voice belonged to a boy or a girl? How?

Did the person giggle or give other clues? If so, what were they?

Did the person have an accent? What words were said differently?

Did the person have a high voice or a low voice?

Did the person have a soft voice or a loud voice?

What other words could be used to talk about different voices?

Write the children's responses on the chalkboard.

ASSESSMENT   Individually, ask the children to listen carefully to a recorded voice and tell you about the voice. Note the elaboration of their responses (how many of the questions in Step 3 they volunteered and the number of different words they used in their description).

Notes for next time . . .

_____

_____

_____

_____

_____

_____

_____

Rebus Rhymes

SUGGESTED GRADE LEVEL *K–1*

PURPOSE
Being able to identify the rhyming element in a word (early phonemic aware-ness) is a first step toward becoming ready for phonics instruction. This activity asks the children to identify rhymes in one-syllable words and to construct their own rhyme cards with matching pictures (rebus cards), as well as act out the pictures. This makes the activity an ideal multisensory experience for English language learners as well.

MATERIALS
- Rebus chart
- Cards with pictures of rhyming elements (from magazines)
- Blank 3 × 5 cards for children to make their own rebus cards

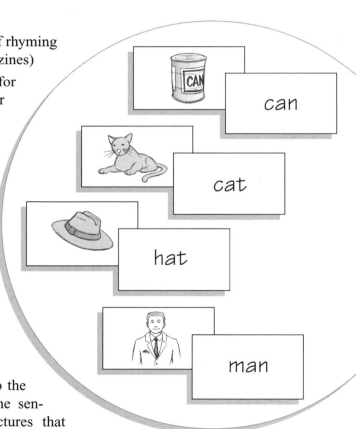

PROCEDURE

1. Discuss with the children that rhyming words are words with the same ending sounds. Give enough examples so the chil-dren are familiar with the concept (examples: cat/hat; man/can; get/wet). Display charts showing sentences with rebus pic-tures illustrating the words for rhyming (see illustration).

2. Introduce the rebus rhyming chart to the class. Explain that you will read the sen-tences and the class will find pictures that rhyme with the picture in each sentence. Have the children watch as you read the first sentence. For example, encourage them to look at the pictures on the individual cards and select the pictures that rhyme with cat. Ask them if they can think of other words that rhyme with cat.

3. Continue reading the rest of the rebus chart, selecting appropriate rhyming pictures and having the children identify other words that rhyme with the picture.

4. In a follow-up lesson, show the children how to make their own rebus game. Create another rebus chart story and encourage the children to draw pictures, on cards, of items that rhyme with the rebus pictures in your story. Optional: You could make another rebus chart as a group activity.

5. Finally, play a pantomime game with the rebus cards. Group the children into teams of three to act out rhyming words. One child from the team is chosen to be "it." That child might draw the card "mop," for example. The child might tell the group that the word rhymes with "top." The other children on the team whose turn it is then must guess the word and act it out. For example, the word "mop" might be acted out by having team members pretend to swab the floor.

ASSESSMENT   After modeling the concept of rhyming for the children, ask each child to provide two rhymes for some common three and four letter words. As a resource, use Rimes and Common Words Containing Them from Appendix E (*SAB,* p. 288).

Notes for next time . . .

_____

_____

_____

_____

_____

_____

_____

_____

_____

The [man] has on a [hat]. The [cat] ate food from a [can]. You [can] get wet when it rains.

Flannelboard Rimes

SUGGESTED GRADE LEVEL *K–1*

PURPOSE

To become ready for the recognition of common word patterns, children first need to be able to hear isolated sounds in words, such as "rimes," or the ending parts of words. This activity allows children to listen for common rimes and then manipulate colorful flannelboard characters to actively participate in creating a story containing many rhyming words.

MATERIALS

- A flannelboard consisting of a 3-foot × 4-foot piece of tagboard covered with flannel
- Three similar characters made of flannel—two boys and a girl
- Another character made of flannel—a man
- A can, a van, and a pan made of flannel

PROCEDURE

1. Start a discussion about word endings by introducing the triplets Nan, Jan, and Dan on the flannelboard.

2. Ask the children to tell you how the names of these three characters are alike. Tell the children that these three characters want to find other words that rhyme with their names.

3. Introduce the story "The Plan of Nan, Jan, and Dan" (below). Ask the children to listen carefully with their eyes closed and to raise their hand every time they hear a word that rhymes with Nan, Jan, and Dan.

Nan, Jan, and Dan

The Plan of Nan, Jan, and Dan

Nan, Jan, and Dan were triplets. One day they saw a strange man. He was selling something in a can. It was something tan.

None of the triplets had money, but they wanted to know what was in the can. Jan said, "I have a plan. Let's pick some berries in this pan. We will trade the berries for what the man has in the can." The others agreed. They ran after the man. Too late! The man had left in a van.

4. Ask the children to say the words they heard that rhyme with Nan, Jan, and Dan. Write the words on the chalkboard or add them to a Word Wall.

5. Invite the children, in groups of four, to act out the story as you reread it. Assign each child to become one of the four characters by manipulating the corresponding character on the flannelboard. Ask the other children to raise their hand every time they hear a word that rhymes with Nan, Jan, or Dan.

6. After all the children who wish to do so have had a chance to participate, ask individual children to retell the story while you manipulate the flannelboard.

ASSESSMENT   Give each child the key word "Nan." Tell the children that the word "can" rhymes with "Nan." Then ask them to say as many other rhyming words from the story as they can remember.

Notes for next time . . .

_____

_____

_____

_____

_____

_____

_____

Flexible Listening

SUGGESTED
GRADE LEVEL   *1–2*

PURPOSE

This activity allows children to experience the range of possible purposes for listening and to begin to adjust their attentiveness to the task at hand. This activity can provide prerequisite listening skills necessary for following directions and obtaining content material through active listening.

MATERIALS

- An audiotape of a conversation (for passive listening)
- A set of directions (for attentive listening)
- A short expository paragraph (for directed listening)
- A humorous short story (for appreciative listening)

PROCEDURE

1. While the children are involved in a seatwork activity, play the audiotaped conversation at a low volume without calling the children's attention to it. When the children have finished their seatwork, ask if they can tell what the taped conversation was about (most will not be able to give a complete account of the conversation). Discuss the type of listening the children were doing as they passively listened to the tape with no given purpose. Help the children create a list of times when they are engaged in *passive listening*. Discussion questions: When is this kind of listening acceptable and appropriate? When is passive listening inappropriate and not acceptable? Tell the children they now will learn about several other kinds of listening and ask them to be thinking about when each might be appropriate.

2. To explain why *attentive listening* is necessary, give the children step-by-step oral instructions for drawing an object without first telling them what the object is (see illustration). When you have finished the directions, ask the children to show what they have drawn. Ask them: Why was it important to listen carefully? What is special about this kind of listening? When might this kind of listening be important?

3. Next, set a purpose (*directed listening*) for the children to listen to a short expository paragraph. The purpose might be to listen for a main idea (Listen to find out reasons why spiders make webs), or for an important supporting detail (Listen to find out how you can tell the difference between a spider and an insect). Read the paragraph aloud. Ask the children: What were you listening for? How did knowing what to listen for help you with your drawing? How can this kind of listening be important?

4. Before reading a humorous short story to the children, tell them they will have an opportunity to share their favorite part with the group after they have listened to it. After the *appreciative listening* experience, invite the children to tell about what part they enjoyed most and why. Discuss this type of listening with the class and have them say what is special about just listening to a story for enjoyment. Ask the children: When would this kind of listening be important? When would it not be appropriate? Why?

5. After the children have been exposed to each of these types of listening, review with them the purposes of each, the limitations of each, and the personal requirements and responsibilities for each type of listening.

The following example can be used for the attentive listening activity (Note: Read slowly and distinctly, but tell the children you will not repeat any of the instructions):

Get out a piece of paper and a pencil and put these on top of your desk. Draw a circle the size of an orange in the middle of your paper. Draw a smaller circle above the larger circle so the bottom of the smaller circle touches the top of the bottom circle. Put a triangle on the top of the smaller circle, but over to one side. Put another triangle on the top of the smaller circle, but over to the other side. Put four sausage shapes at the bottom of the larger circle with the smallest parts touching the bottom of the big circle. Put one more sausage shape on the side of the larger circle with the small part touching the side of the larger circle.

The drawing should look something like this:

ASSESSMENT As the children are listening to the instructions and doing their drawings, go around the room with a clipboard, taking anecdotal notes on your observations of the ability of each child to listen carefully and follow the instructions. The drawings also can be assessed for accuracy and compared with drawings done with instructions given at a later date to determine growth in attentive listening.

Other Ideas & Activities

● **PICTURE CAPTIONS**

After each child draws a picture, have him or her tell you about it so you can print one or two sentences below it. Then read the sentences back to the child.

● **I'M GOING TO BETSY'S**

Play this game with the children. Have the first child begin by saying, I'm going to Betsy's and I will take a ball. Ask the next player to repeat that sentence, replacing the word "ball" with another word that begins with the same sound. Continue until no one can think of another word with that sound. Then work with another beginning sound (I'm going to Carol's and I will take a cow).

● **EXCURSIONS**

Take your students on brief excursions (walks around the school, park, playground, shopping trips, visits to the park, farm, firehouse, zoo, and so forth). Discuss these adventures with the students to increase their vocabulary and choice of words. When community members have been involved, write a collaborative thank-you note to that person using the LEA (see Chapter 3) format.

● **TELEVISION DISCUSSIONS**

Assign television programs with educational value. The next day discuss them with your students. Ask questions that require children to think: Why do you think? What might have happened if . . . ? How did it make you feel when . . . ? Pursue the interest generated by programs with follow-up reading.

● **MODEL READING**

Read something (the newspaper, a novel, a magazine article, a how-to book, etc.) in the presence of your students every day, preferably during Free Reading time when they are engaged in browsing through books.

● **VISIT TO THE LIBRARY**

Visit the school library as often as possible. Help the children select books of interest to them as well as books you can read aloud to them. Acquire a classroom library where books can be checked out. Include books for all interest and ability levels and books of all cultures and genres.

● **BOOKS FROM OTHER SOURCES**

Obtain books through book fairs and book clubs. If you have Internet access, web sites such as www.amazon.com and www.barnesandnoble.com., have massive collections of children's books and recommendations. Also, Chinaberry Book Service, a mail-order children's book service, will send a highly imaginative and descriptive catalog anywhere in the world (1-800-776-2242).

- **MAGIC WORD**

  Play this enjoyable game, in which everyone agrees on a magic word. During free time when children are conversing, ask your students to listen for the magic word. The first one to raise a hand when hearing the word gets a point. The person with the most points wins.

- **DAILY READING**

  Read to the children every day. To get an idea of what to read, use the Reading Teacher's Children's Choice Award Winners from *The Reading Teacher* or Newbery Winners.

- **MOVABLE BOOKS**

  For children who have trouble sitting still to listen to a story, try movable books. These books, such as Eric Carle's *The Very Hungry Caterpillar* and *The Very Quiet Cricket,* move, flip, or have texture, keeping active young children engaged.

- **WORDLESS BOOKS**

  Sometimes select wordless books. These books, such as *The Bear and the Fly* by Paula Winter, show a story through the pictures, allowing children to increase their oral language by telling the story in their own words.

- **BOOKS ON TAPE**

  Tape-record some of your students' favorite books so they can hear these whenever they wish. Although listening to a tape cannot replace a shared reading experience, this is a great solution for the teacher in a time crunch. As an alternative to taping stories yourself, many fine stories are available commercially, recorded by celebrities such as Cher, Meryl Streep, and Robin Williams as narrators.

Children's Literature List

Baker, Alan. *I Thought I Heard: A Book of Noises.* (Brookfield, CT: Copper Beech, 1996).

A sleeping child awakens to scary noises. By shining a flashlight around the room, she discovers that a clock, the cat, and a moth are making the noises. The repetition of, "I thought I heard . . ." and "it really was . . ." combined with the attention to environmental sounds, makes this an ideal book for preliterate children.

Berends, Polly Berrien. *"I Heard," Said the Bird.* (New York: Dial, 1995).

Hearing that a new animal was coming, the other animals wondered what it was. They learned from a boy that the new one is a baby. Repeated lines provide an opportunity for choral or shared reading and also for predicting what the new animal is.

Kirk, David. *Miss Spider's ABC.* (New York: Scholastic, 1998).

Miss Spider's active alphabetical friends plan a surprise birthday party for her. This lovely book can be used to reinforce the letters of the alphabet in order in a most enjoyable way.

Schertle, Alice, illustrated by E. B. Lewis. *Down the Road.* (New York: Browndeer/Harcourt Brace, 1995).

Hetty is going to the store by herself for the first time. When she breaks the eggs she has purchased, she climbs a tree to think. The language of sound words, vivid descriptive words and phrases, and lovely verbs makes this an excellent book for reading aloud to young children.

Weninger, Brigitte. *Ragged Bear.* (New York: North-South, 1996).

A tattered teddy bear's rescue and repair by a loving child is portrayed in delightful water-color illustrations. This tender childhood classic tale could be preceded by a "picture walk" to discuss book components and predict what might happen.

Other Resources for Developing Early Literacy

Beyond Storybooks: Young Children and the Shared Book Experience, by Judith Pollard Slaughter (Newark, DE: International Reading Association, 1993).

A practical, hands-on book for people working with emergent readers in preschool and kindergarten. Initial shared book experiences with Big Books versions of favorite predictable stories leads children to develop awareness of various concepts about print. An annotated bibliography of more than 100 children's books is included.

Facilitating Preschool Literacy, by Robin Campbell, editor (Newark, DE: International Reading Association, 1998).

Considers the notion of young children constructing literacy; looks at literacy in the context of home and family; and presents ways to provide support for children as they begin the rudimentary tasks of beginning to read and write.

Linking Literacy and Play, by Kathleen A. Roskos, Carol Vukelich, James F. Christie, Billie J. Enz, and Susan B. Neuman (Newark, DE: International Reading Association, 1998).

This video and facilitator's guide provides early childhood teachers, parents, and caregivers with ideas about how to use the natural environment and environmental print to foster emerging concepts about print, combining literacy with play.

Literacy in the Pre-School: The Roles of Teachers and Parents, by Bronwyn Reynolds (Herndon, VA: Stylus Publishing, 1997).

An observation of the awareness children have about the relevance of signs, labels, notices, and directions. The author relates her experiences to theories of early learning and how concepts about print are acquired.

The Reading Environment: How Adults Help Children Enjoy Books, by Aidan Chambers (York, ME: Stenhouse Publishers, 1996).

Concerned with practical aspects of creating an environment that supports young children as they begin to make sense of print. The author provides a multitude of stimulating ideas for introducing the pleasures of literacy to children.

Starting Out Right: A Guide to Promoting Children's Reading Success, by M. Susan Burns, Peg Griffin, and Catherine E. Snow (Newark, DE: International Reading Association, 1999).

Simplifies research findings to practical guidelines and suggestions and provides many ideas and examples about how to introduce children to print most effectively.

In Closing

1. After using the activities in this section, what insights have you gained about how children develop emergent literacy? What did you discover about yourself as a teacher of literacy by teaching these activities?

2. Which of the following activities do you think were particularly effective for reinforcing the following concepts about print? Why?

   - Understanding that text carries meaning

   - Ability to point to letters, words, and sentences

   - Understanding that text proceeds from left to right, top to bottom

   - Ability to identify punctuation

   - Understanding the parts of a story

3. Which activity do you think was the most effective in helping to develop the following skills? Why?

   - Vocabulary

   - Listening

   - Working cooperatively

   - Organizing ideas

   - Responding to literature

   - Experimenting with language

4. What did you discover about the need to determine what children already know about a concept before beginning an instructional activity? How did the assessment suggestions at the end of each activity provide you with insights into the strengths and limitations of your teaching of emergent literacy?

5. Select an activity that offered you the most insight into the literacy background of your learners. What did you discover? Cite examples of specific children with whom you worked.

6. Several of the activities asked you to transcribe words or sentences composed by a group of students. What concepts about print were reinforced as a result of these activities?

7. Several of the activities invited children to dramatize stories or role-play certain characters. How was early literacy developed through participation in these activities? Give some examples of specific children and what you think they learned as a result of this dramatic play.

8. Some activities asked children to draw pictures of events, objects, or people in their lives. What might be the advantages or disadvantages of such activities? What did you learn about a specific child's understanding of story structure based upon these drawings?

9. Which activities were difficult for ELL children? What did you observe about their difficulties? How could you revise these activities for them?

10. Identify a child you think has highly developed language ability. What are the characteristics of that child? Did his or her behavior during the activities differ from that of other children? Describe the differences, if any.

2

ACTIVITIES TO DEVELOP PHONEMIC AWARENESS

Introduction

Phonemic awareness, the construction of a bridge between spoken and written language, is an important link to oral language understanding. A child who has a high level of phonemic awareness can segment and manipulate sounds in words, blend strings of isolated sounds together to form recognizable words, and tell where one word ends and another one begins. Phonemic awareness has been shown to be a crucial foundation for later instruction in phonics, or the relationship between sounds and letters. When integrated into a program rich with language and print, early instruction in phonemic awareness is often the instructional component that allows teachers to teach every child to read—even children who historically have fallen through the cracks.

Research suggests that phonemic awareness activities can maximize children's potential for a successful learning-to-read experience. Therefore, teachers of kindergarten and first-grade children should spend a few minutes each day engaging children in oral language activities that explicitly emphasize the sequence of sounds in the English language. The following activities have been chosen to do just that.

Counting Words

(Adapted from Cunningham & Allington, 1994)

1

SUGGESTED GRADE LEVEL *K–1*

PURPOSE

Through this enjoyable activity, children learn to separate words in speech, which is an initial task in phonemic awareness. They also practice critical oral counting skills.

MATERIALS

- 10 items for each child, to be used as counters (beans, popcorn, blank tiles, raisins, etc.)
- Sentence strips, prewritten
- A square of colored paper, 8 inches × 8 inches for each child

PROCEDURE

1. Pass out 10 counters and a colored square to each child.

2. Begin by asking the children to help you count some common objects, such as several paperclips or pictures on the wall. Have the children put one of their counters on their colored square for each item counted.

3. Tell the children that you can count words in the same way. Explain that you will say a sentence once and then repeat it slowly, word by word. The children are to put a counter on the colored square for each word in the sentence. Begin with short sentences of no more than three words (example: The man laughed), and gradually lengthen the sentences (Everyone liked the story we heard yesterday).

4. After each child has decided on the number of counters needed for the sentence, show each of them the sentence strip and have them count the words with you as you point to each word, moving from left to right. Make anecdotal notes of children who are having problems with this activity for later review.

5. As the children become proficient at this activity, encourage them to make up sentences for their classmates, saying them slowly, one word at a time, as they count them.

ASSESSMENT   Individually, read a five-, six-, and seven-word sentence. For each, ask the child to tell how many words are in the sentence. Record the information and place in the child's file.

Notes for next time . . .

Count words on fingers, spaces between each
finger represent the space between words.

Sound Boxes

2

SUGGESTED
GRADE LEVEL *K–1*

PURPOSE   By segmenting sounds and marking them on a sound box, children will develop one-to-one correspondence with a beginning, middle, and ending sound that make up a word.

MATERIALS
- Picture of familiar objects containing one or two sounds (examples: man, hat, pen, fish, boat, cane, dog)
- Tagboard rectangles, divided into three sections (see illustration).
- Three markers for each participant

PROCEDURE

1. Pass out three markers and a tagboard rectangle to each child.

2. Show the children the picture of the man and ask them to tell you what is in the picture. Tell them you are going to pretend the word is a rubberband and you are going to stretch it out. Have them say with you, "Mmmmmm-maaaaaaannnnnnn."

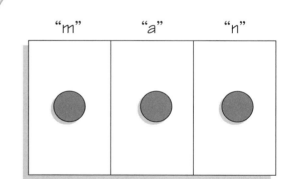

3. Tell them that for each different sound they hear, you are going to put a marker on your tagboard sound box and they are to do the same. Demonstrate this by putting a marker in the first square for /m/, a marker in the second square for /a/, and a marker in the third square for /n/.

4. Ask the children to say the word slowly as they put a finger on each sound in the box as it is intoned.

5. Continue this procedure with the rest of the words the pictures represent. Adapt this activity to meet the needs of differing ability levels by using fewer sections for words with only two

sounds (e.g., me, go, at) or made more challenging by using four or more boxes for words containing four or more sounds (e.g., clown, frog, train, bottle).

ASSESSMENT   Check competency for segmenting by asking the children individually to mark their sound box for 10 words, beginning with two-sound words and stopping when the task becomes too difficult for them.

Notes for next time . . .

Give kids rubber bands to "stretch" out the sounds of each word

It's My Name!

ACTIVITIES TO DEVELOP PHONEMIC AWARENESS

SUGGESTED GRADE LEVEL *K–1*

PURPOSE

Through this activity, children can begin to understand the concept of *word,* that names are words, that words can be written, and that it takes lots of letters to write them. Finally, highlighting one child each day will boost self-esteem.

MATERIALS

- Box with cover
- Strips of paper each containing the name of a child in the class
- Blank strips
- Drawing paper
- Colorful cardboard crown (optional)

PROCEDURE

1. Reach into the box and draw out the name of a child in the class. Crown that child (optional).

2. Invite other children in the class to interview the child, asking, for example: Do you have a pet? What are your favorite activities? Foods? and so forth.

3. Call children's attention to the child's name, *Ramona,* as you point to the name strip, saying, "This word is *Ramona.* A name can be a word." Ask the children if the word is a short one or a long one. Tell the children it takes many letters to write the word *Ramona.* Ask the children to help you count the number of letters in this word.

4. Say the letters in *Ramona* one by one while pointing to each, and have the children chant them with you. Take a blank strip and have the children chant the spelling of the letters for you as you write them.

5. Give each child a large sheet of drawing paper and invite the children to draw a picture of the highlighted child—in this case, Ramona. Ask them to write the word *Ramona* underneath. Model on the board how to write each letter as they copy it. Optionally: With the class, brainstorm some words that begin like the first sound in the child's name. Place these words on a Word Wall.

6. On subsequent days, repeat this procedure with the name of another child in the class. Continue with the activity every day until all of the children's names have been highlighted.

ASSESSMENT   Spot-check the children's competency in differentiating long and short words by asking each child individually to tell you whether a word you say is a long one or a short one. If they are unsure, write out the word in front of them and ask them to count the number of letters.

Notes for next time . . .

_____

_____

_____

_____

_____

_____

_____

_____

_____

_____

_____

Toe Tappers

SUGGESTED
GRADE LEVEL *K–1*

PURPOSE Tapping sounds is rhythmic fun for children. Furthermore, it is effective, re-quires little time, and entails no preparation or materials on your part. Tapping sounds helps learners become aware of the individual sounds in words. They are learning to segment words into their discrete, sequential sounds, an important phonemic-awareness task.

MATERIALS
- None
- Optional: pencil for each learner

PROCEDURE

1. Demonstrate for the children how to tap by saying a short word slowly, segmenting the two sounds and tapping your toe for each sound. Example: By: /b/ – /y/. In this example you would tap your toe only twice to indicate the two sounds.

2. Invite the learners to do the tapping. Begin with two-sound words (such as me, go, by, on, so, at), carefully seg-menting the sounds so the children can hear each sound and tap once for each sound they hear.

3. Repeat the same words two or three times initially to make sure the children get the idea.

4. As the children gain proficiency, say the words slowly only once.

5. Introduce words with three sounds, and eventually four, stretching them out as above.

Toe Tappers

Continued.

Variation

Instead of toe tapping, distribute a pencil to each child and allow the children to tap each sound on their desk.

ASSESSMENT   Assess each child individually by asking him or her to tap a toe to two-sound, then three-sound words, and finally to three- and four-sound words. Note where problems occur.

Notes for next time . . .

_____

_____

_____

_____

_____

_____

_____

_____

_____

_____

_____

_____

_____

_____

_____

Speaking Martian

SUGGESTED GRADE LEVEL *K–1*

PURPOSE

The children can practice the phonemic awareness task of blending sounds together to make words through this engaging activity. By listening to a series of longer and longer words stretched out in an exaggerated fashion, they will begin to understand that each word contains a sequence of sounds.

MATERIALS

- A list of words containing two sounds
- A list of words containing three sounds
- Optional: a puppet resembling a friendly Martian

"Stretching" or "rubber-banding" a word

PROCEDURE

mmmmmmmaaaaaaaannnnnnnn

1. Introduce the puppet to the children, explaining that it speaks a language that at first may seem strange but is a language that it hopes all the children will quickly learn to speak.

2. Tell the children that the puppet will say a word in the Martian language. The word will be just like a word they know, but they must "snap" the sounds together quickly to figure out what the word might be.

3. Have the puppet say the first word in an exaggerated, stretched-out manner ("Mmmmmmmaaaaaaaannnnnnnnn"), to which the children must blend the sounds into the word *man,* quickly.

4. Have the puppet slowly say all the rest of the words on the two lists in this manner while the children try to blend the sounds the puppet is saying in its "Martian language."

5 *Speaking Martian*

Continued.

5. Invite children who think they have mastered the Martian language to come up and say a word in Martian for the other children to guess. Ask each child to first tell the word to the puppet to have it determine if the word is indeed Martian.

ASSESSMENT   Take anecdotal notes on who is and who is not able to blend the words, being sure to give every child a turn. To assess the ability to segment, invite all the children to take a turn at saying a word in Martian (segmenting).

Notes for next time . . .

_____

_____

_____

_____

_____

_____

_____

_____

_____

_____

_____

_____

_____

_____

Parts of the Body

ACTIVITIES TO DEVELOP PHONEMIC AWARENESS

SUGGESTED GRADE LEVEL *K–1*

PURPOSE Through this activity, which uses an engaging story together with a physical activity, the children will begin to recognize the beginning parts (onsets) and ending parts (rimes) of words. English language learners will learn names for parts of the body.

MATERIALS
- *Tog the Dog,* by C. Hawkins and J. Hawkins
- Picture cards upon which are drawn parts of the body (hand, leg, arm, foot, toe, waist, neck, head, nose)

PROCEDURE

1. Explain to the children that you are going to play a game using words from parts of the body. Show the children the picture cards one at a time and have them chant the names of the body parts while pointing to them on their own body as they are depicted.

2. Tell the children you are going to put two sounds together to make one of the words we just said. Say: I will say the beginning sound of a word and then the rest of the word. The first part I hear at the beginning of the word *leg* is /l/. I hear /eg/ at the end of the word. /l/ and /eg/: (pause) leg. Say it with me. Leg. (Have the children repeat the steps of the procedure with the word *leg.*)

3. Using all the picture cards, have the children segment and then blend all the body-part words just as they did in Step 2. As the word is finally blended together, encourage the children to hold up, shake, or point to their body part.

4. Read *Tog the Dog* to the children. Encourage them to interact with the onsets and rimes in the story using the above steps by calling attention to new words as you turn each page.

⑥ *Parts of the Body*

Continued.

ASSESSMENT   Individually, have children point to a part of their body and segment it as they did in the activity. Anecdotally, note strengths and needs and place the notes in the child's file.

Notes for next time . . .

_____

_____

_____

_____

_____

_____

_____

_____

_____

_____

_____

_____

_____

_____

_____

_____

_____

_____

_____

_____

Shopping for Sounds

**SUGGESTED
GRADE LEVEL**   *K–1*

PURPOSE   This enjoyable language-play activity can enhance the ability to hear and manipulate beginning sounds, or onsets, or, alternatively, to hear and manipulate ending sounds, or rimes. English language learners will be able to participate in the game because of its repetitive nature and the use of concrete objects.

MATERIALS
- Shopping bag with many items that have the same beginning sound (onset) or ending sound (rime)

PROCEDURE

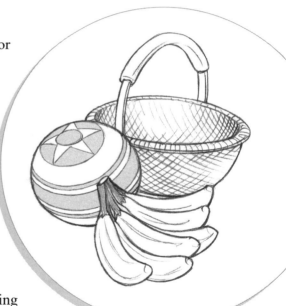

1. Create an alliterative shopping bag full of six items or so, all beginning with the same first letter or letter combination. Example: bean, banana, basket, book, balloon, ball, biscuit, baby food.

2. Explain to the children that you are all going to go on a pretend shopping trip to the store and you will pretend to take home the items in the bag.

3. Start the game by holding up one of the objects and saying, "I went to the store and I bought a bean," exaggerating the initial /b/ in bean. Have children repeat this sentence.

4. Ask a volunteer to select an object from the shopping bag and create a new cumulative sentence, adding the new object to the previous one: "I went to the store and I bought a bean and a banana," while holding up the banana and pointing to the bean. Invite the rest of the class to repeat the sentence after the child.

5. Continue recruiting volunteers to select new objects, and add them to those that have been mentioned previously, pointing to each object as it is mentioned. If the children forget an object, have the child who is holding that object hold it up as a reminder.

6. When all the objects have been used, ask the children if they can think of any other objects that begin with the same sound.

7 *Shopping for Sounds*

Continued.

7. After the children become proficient with beginning sounds they remember in this manner, do the same activity using objects that rhyme. Example: boat, coat, note, goat; or fan, man, can, pan. Or, try the game with ending sounds that are the same. Example: card, head, bed, sand.

ASSESSMENT   Assess the children one at a time. Show them an object from this activity. Ask them to name as many items as they can think of that begin with the same sound.

Notes for next time . . .

_____

_____

_____

_____

_____

_____

_____

_____

_____

_____

_____

_____

_____

_____

_____

_____

_____

Camel Chant

SUGGESTED GRADE LEVEL *K–1*

PURPOSE
This advanced phonemic awareness activity requires children to chant or sing a whimsical rhyming poem and then change the beginning sound or sounds of the rhyme to correspond to the beginning sound or sounds of a classmate's name. The repetition allows all children to catch on, at their own rate, to the idea of initial sound substitution.

MATERIALS
- Camel poem in large letters on chart paper
- Toy or stuffed camel (optional)

PROCEDURE

1. Tell the children they are going to learn a short poem about a camel. The first part of the poem will remain the same, but they are to change the second part by using the name of a classmate of their choice.

2. Teach the children the first part of the poem by saying it once for them while pointing to the words on the chart, then having them echo each line, and finally saying or singing the four lines together:

   Bibbety bobbety bee,
   The camel is looking at ME!
   Bibbety bobbety boo,
   The camel is looking at YOU!

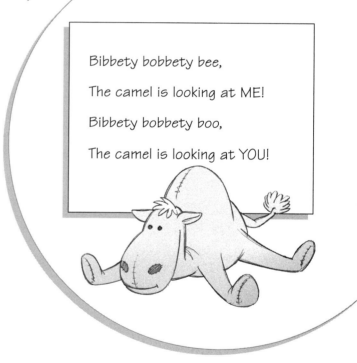

Bibbety bobbety bee,

The camel is looking at ME!

Bibbety bobbety boo,

The camel is looking at YOU!

3. Review the concept of rhyme with the children. Ask them to tell which words in the poem rhyme.

4. Teach the children the remainder of the verse. Tell them: In the last part of the poem, the camel is looking at someone in the class and we must make the poem rhyme with that child's name. Let's use Sally as an example:

Continued.

> Bibbety bobbety Bally,
> The camel is looking at Sally!

5. Now tell the children: Let's say the whole poem together and in the last part have the camel look at Tiffany. Chant the poem as follows:

> Bibbety bobbety bee,
> The camel is looking at ME!
> Bibbety bobbety boo,
> The camel is looking at YOU!
>
> Bibbety bobbety Biffany,
> The camel is looking at Tiffany!

6. Tell the children it is now Tiffany's turn. Class members will say the first part of the poem together, and then Tiffany must choose a classmate and rhyme the last word in the next to the last line with the name of the child she chooses. Help the children with this task until they are proficient with substituting beginning sounds.

ASSESSMENT   Be sure each child in the group has a turn. Take anecdotal notes documenting who is able to make the appropriate initial consonant substitutions and who needs more practice.

Notes for next time . . .

_____

_____

_____

_____

_____

_____

Sound Train

(Adapted from a lesson by Karen Gilligan)

**SUGGESTED
GRADE LEVEL** K–1

PURPOSE   Through this delightful phonemic awareness activity, children will gain practice in isolating beginning sounds (onsets). Pictures are used as an aid to English language learners, and collaborative learning is encouraged.

MATERIALS
- Picture cards for beginning sounds
- Whistle

PROCEDURE

1. Seat the class in a circle.

2. Pass out picture cards, one for each child.

3. Ask the children individually to tell their neighbor what object is represented on their card, or to ask for help if they are unsure.

4. You, the teacher, are the "conductor." Blow the whistle and tell the children a letter sound that you know is represented by one of the pictures, saying, "The /m/ train is now boarding for /M/aine. The ticket to get on board is any picture that begins with the /m/ sound." Help the children determine if they have the required picture.

5. Have the children who have the "ticket" form a line and march around the outside of the circle as they make the /m/ sound and you blow the whistle intermittently.

6. As each child circles around to his or her original seat, have him or her say the word one more time, then "exit" the train.

7. Repeat the procedure with other letter sounds, going to places for which the first letter matches the target sound. When all the children understand the game, invite a child to be the "conductor."

ASSESSMENT   As an individual assessment, call each child up to your desk. Lay out all the pictures for the child to see. Articulate a sound and ask the child to find a picture that begins with the sound. Do this for all the sounds represented by the pictures. Note in the child's file any sounds that are causing problems, for future direct instruction.

Notes for next time . . .

_____

_____

_____

_____

_____

_____

_____

_____

_____

_____

_____

_____

_____

Beanbag Toss

**SUGGESTED
GRADE LEVEL** *K–1*

PURPOSE   This phoneme-manipulation activity develops social skills as well as large-motor skills while reinforcing targeted sounds.

MATERIALS   • Beanbag or small stuffed toy

PROCEDURE

**Possible
rhymes to use:**

can, man, Nan,
pan, Jan, tan, ran, fan, Dan

den, men, hen, when, Jen, ten, Len

bite, kite, light, night, sight, right, fight, bright

bug, jug, lug, tug, rug, hug, mug, snug, drug, dug

king, ring, wing, sing, thing, bring, swing, fling

hat, cat, bat, vat, chat, Nat, sat, fat, mat

sit, hit, mitt, bit, flit, wit, fit, pit

got, trot, not, rot, pot, shot,
hot, plot, cot, dot,
jot, lot

1. To reinforce the idea of rhyme, say the following poem to the children and then ask them to repeat it after you, pointing out the two rhyming words:

   > I'll think of a word, I'll give you some time,
   >
   > I'll give you the word, please give me a rhyme.

2. Arrange the children, standing, in a circle. Say the above rhyme together.

3. Explain to the children that you will say the rhyme, say the word, then toss the beanbag to someone in the circle. When that child catches the beanbag, he or she must first say the word, then think of another word that rhymes with it. Offer examples (e.g., man/fan; get/wet) until everyone understands what they are to do.

4. Say the rhyme and then a word that has many rhymes, such as *bug*. Toss the beanbag to a child and ask the child to say the word *bug* and a word that rhymes with it.

5. Instruct the child to choose another child to toss the beanbag to. That child must say the original word, the last child's word, and a new rhyme (nonsense words are acceptable).

6. When all the possible rhymes have been suggested, say the poem, select a new word, and again toss the beanbag to a child.

Variations

After the game is familiar to all, encourage children to lead the game by selecting their own word to rhyme. In addition, use the game to reinforce beginning sounds by changing the rhyme:

> I have a word, I'll give it to you
> You give me a word that starts that way, too.

ASSESSMENT   Make a chart of the rhyming words used in the game. Individually, have the children offer a rhyming word as you give the original word. Check off the words that each child is able to rhyme and those that give each child trouble. Regroup children who have difficulty hearing rhymes at all and provide direct instruction in this skill.

Notes for next time . . .

_____

_____

_____

_____

_____

_____

_____

_____

_____

_____

_____

Other Ideas & Activities

- **JUMPING ROPE CHANTS**
Bring in a jump rope and encourage the children to jump to the chants they use on the playground. Have them listen for the rhyming words.

- **ROLL CALL**
When taking attendance and greeting children in the morning, select a letter they studied the day before and substitute that letter for the beginning sounds of all children (e.g., Mary Jones becomes Bary Bones).

- **NAME THE ANIMALS**
Brainstorm all the animal names the children know. Have them make up rhyming names, such as Trish the fish and Myrtle the turtle.

- **PICTURE SORTS**
Working in small groups, have the children sort magazine pictures on the basis of a selected beginning sound or ending sound.

- **RIDDLES**
Make up riddles giving the children phonemic information as clues. Example: I'm thinking of an animal that has the same ending sound as bat.

- **SOUND BINGO**
Make up bingo cards with pictures of common items. Call out the words. If children have items on their card beginning with the same sound, they place a marker on that picture.

- **TONGUE TWISTERS**
Have the children create tongue twisters by using the names of the children in the class in an alliterative phrase. Example: Mary made a merry monster mess on Monday.

- **SOUND ALERT!**
When reading literature to the children, call attention to words that have interesting sounds (such as pumpernickel). Also, routinely point out words that contain sounds that have been recently introduced.

- **NURSERY RHYMES**
Teach the children common nursery rhymes, calling attention to the rhyming patterns. If you do not play a musical instrument, sing the rhymes along with a recording.

- **I SPY!**
Adapt this popular children's game by asking the children to find an object beginning or ending with a certain letter. Example: I spy with my little eye something beginning with /r/ (radio).

- **LINE UP**

  When releasing children for lunch or recess, have them line up by the beginning sounds of their first names. Example: Line up now if your first name begins with a /p/ sound.

- **PREDICTABLE BOOKS**

  Read the children lots of predictable books in rhyme format, such as *Good Zap, Little Grog* (by Sarah Wilson, 1995). After the children recognize the pattern, have them predict the rhyme. For a list of suitable predictable books, see *SAB,* Appendix C.

- **RAP SONGS**

  Using children's names and events in the classroom, create simple rap songs to which children chant along. The rhyme, rhythm, and repetition helps ELL children tune in to the cadence of the language.

- **NAME REVERSALS**

  Have children practice manipulating beginning sounds by experimenting with the names of the children in the class. For example, "Bobby Jones" becomes "Jobby Bones" as they reverse the beginning sounds of the child's first and last names.

- **SOUND WALK**

  Select a target sound the class has been studying. Take a short walk around the school looking for as many objects as the children can find that begin with that sound. Upon returning to the classroom, see how many objects with the sound the children can remember.

Children's Literature List

Edwards, Pamela Duncan, illustrated by Henry Cole. *Warthogs in the Kitchen: A Sloppy Counting Book.* (New York: Hyperion, 1998).

Eight wild warthogs mix up 10 delicious cupcakes, along with lots of fun and a huge mess. Children will enjoy finishing the rhymes and counting the objects in each illustration.

Hoberman, Mary Ann, illustrated by Nadine Bernard Westcott. *Miss Mary Mack.* (Boston: Little, Brown, 1998).

The classic rhyming chant about Miss Mary Mack and an adventure with an elephant. A hand-clapping game using the words of the rhyme on the inside cover is a great reinforcer for listening to the rhythm of our language as well as rhyme.

Robinson, Marc, illustrated by Steve Jenkins. *Cock-a-Doodle-Do! What Does It Sound Like to You?* (New York: Stewart, Tabori, & Chang, 1993).

A lively, rhythmic text exploring the onomatopoeic sounds of animals, trains, and even dripping water in some of the world's languages. The book can provide a multicultural component as children listen for different interpretations of sounds for items they know.

Sturges, Philemon, illustrated by Joan Paley. *What's That Sound, Woolly Bear?* (Boston: Little, Brown, 1996).

A simple story about a bear that tries to find a quiet place to sleep among many insects that make an assortment of noises, from "slish, slash," to "dash, dart." Full of playful language that can help children tune into beginning consonants and consonant blends.

Other Resources for Developing Phonemic Awareness

Assessing and Teaching Phonological Knowledge, by J. Munro (Herndon, VA: Stylus Publishing, 1998).

Tests that enable teachers to decide whether a child's lack of phonological knowledge is contributing to reading difficulties and then to plan and implement a teaching-support system for children who need it.

Classrooms That Work: They Can All Read and Write, 2d edition, by Patricia M. Cunningham and Richard L. Allington (New York: Longman, 1999).

A plethora of ideas for developing readers, writers, and thinkers using a variety of authentic narrative and expository texts. The authors share the viewpoint that phonics instruction is necessary, but it is not enough to create joyful readers who construct their own meaning from text.

Phonemic Awareness in Young Children, by Marilyn Jager Adams, Barbara R. Foorman, Ingvar Lundberg, and Terri Beeler (Baltimore: Paul H. Brookes Publishing, 1998).

A supplemental language and reading program to complement any prereading program with an entire year's worth of enjoyable and adaptable games and activities for rhyming, segmenting, and manipulating sounds.

Phonemic Awareness: Playing with Sounds to Strengthen Beginning Reading Skills, by Jo Fitzpatrick (Cypress, CA: Creative Teaching Press, 1997).

A compendium of activities to help children become aware of the sequences of sounds in words—lesson plans, activity adaptations, and troubleshooting guidelines.

The Phonological Awareness Handbook for Kindergarten and Primary Teachers, by Lita Ericson and Moira Fraser Juliebo (Newark, DE: International Reading Association, 1998).

Offers a practical and comprehensive means of teaching and monitoring children's development of phonological awareness in the classroom. The authors provide answers to frequently asked questions about phonological awareness, offer a possible teaching sequence, and suggest a variety of activities to enhance these important skills.

A Sound Way, by Elizabeth Love and Sue Reilly (Bothell, WA: Wright Group, 1998).

Provides explicit ways to help children acquire clear concepts of sounds and letters and the critical association between the two.

In Closing

1. After using the activities in this section, what insights have you gained about how children develop phonemic awareness? What did you discover about yourself as a teacher of literacy by teaching these activities?

2. Which of the activities did you find particularly helpful in reinforcing the following skills related to phonemic awareness:

   - Awareness of words

   - Ability to rhyme

   - Ability to blend

   - Ability to segment

   - Ability to identify beginning sounds

   - Ability to substitute and manipulate beginning sounds

   - Ability to substitute middle and ending sounds

3. What did you discover about the need to determine what children already know about phonemic awareness before beginning a new instructional activity? How did the assessment suggestions at the end of each activity provide you with insights into the strengths and limitations of your teaching of phonemic awareness?

4. Select an activity that offered you the most insights into the phonemic awareness backgrounds of your learners. What did you discover? Cite examples of specific children with whom you worked.

5. Choose an activity that was difficult and one that was easy for your learners. Why do you think it was difficult/easy? What, if any, adaptations would you make the next time you teach the lesson?

6. Several of the activities asked you to sing or chant repetitive phrases with the children. What did these activities teach children about phonemic awareness? What did you discover about a specific child's phonemic awareness as a result of these activities?

7. Some activities asked the children to count words or syllables. Describe why you think these activities may be effective prerequisites to eventual instruction in phonics.

8. Several activities combined language play with a physical activity. How did the children respond to these types of activities? What are the advantages and disadvantages of these activities?

9. Which activities were especially difficult for your ELL children? What did you observe about their difficulties? How could you revise these activities for your ELL children?

10. Identify a child whom you think has a highly developed ability to hear and manipulate sounds. What are the characteristics of that child? Did his or her behavior during the activities differ from that of the other children? Describe the differences, if any. What instructional adaptations will you make for this child in future phonemic-awareness lessons?

ACTIVITIES FOR PHONICS INSTRUCTION

Introduction

Phonics is the study of the relationship between the letters in written words and the sounds in spoken words. Whenever you are helping readers decipher our alphabetic writing system, you are teaching phonics. This system of representing sounds with symbols is called the *alphabetic principle.* When applying the alphabetic principle to unknown words, the reader blends a series of sounds dictated by the sequence of the letters in the printed word. When the children are able to do this successfully, they are able to decode or unlock the code necessary to understand written language.

In general, proficient readers are better able than poor readers to use the alphabetic code. Research has shown this to be true in the early grades as well as in the later grades. Though reading entails more than being able to decode well, its contribution to reading with adequate comprehension is critical. Moreover, strong evidence suggests that children who develop efficient decoding strategies quickly find reading enjoyable and thus read more. Conversely, children who get off to a slow start in learning how to decode words rarely catch up to become strong readers who choose the activity.

The following activities have been selected to reinforce children's experience with the relationship between sounds and letters. The first part is composed of activities that will enhance the emerging phonics knowledge of all children in a class. The second part contains activities that also have vocabulary acquisition components and thus are expressly designed for the needs of the English language learner. The last part presents more challenging activities for children who possess rudimentary decoding skills.

Picture Dictionary

SUGGESTED
GRADE LEVEL *K–1*

PURPOSE
By experimenting with pictures that begin with all the sounds of the alphabet, one at a time, the children will gain practice in matching sounds to symbols and create a picture dictionary. Moreover, children for whom English is a second language will enhance their vocabulary at the same time.

MATERIALS
- A supply of pictures, which can be secured from workbooks, magazines, catalogs, and the like
- Large pieces of white construction paper for each group
- Glue or paste
- Scissors

PROCEDURE

1. Introduce a letter sound such as /b/ by having the children repeat the words *ball, baby,* and *bag* after you.

2. Ask the children if they can tell you what is the same about each of the three words.

3. Explain that each word begins with the same sound and that sound is /b/. Write the letter *b* on the board. Explain that this letter goes with the sound /b/.

4. Distribute construction paper, scissors, paste, and pictures to small groups of children.

5. Model how to write the letter *b* on the top of a piece of construction paper. Ask the groups to select one member each to write a letter *b* on the top of their paper.

6. Explain to the children that they now will look through their pictures for some animals, objects, and other items that begin with a *b*. When they think they have found one, they are to

barn   basket

bed   boat

book   bird

Continued.

discuss it with their group and, if all agree, they will paste it on their paper. Ask them to then write below the picture a *b* and other letters they hear in the word (demonstrate this sounding-out process for them). Tell them you will be coming around to answer any questions.

7. Follow the same procedure with subsequent letters as they are introduced.

ASSESSMENT   Ask individual children from each group to share their picture dictionaries with you. Have them tell you the letter and tell the names of the items on the page(s) that begin with the letter. Note any difficulties with specific sounds anecdotally and place them in the child's file.

Notes for next time . . .

_____

_____

_____

_____

_____

_____

_____

_____

_____

_____

_____

_____

_____

Word Wall Detective

SUGGESTED
GRADE LEVEL   *1–2*

PURPOSE   Word Walls are particularly effective for teaching the high-frequency words children will need in their everyday writing and spelling. This activity can be used to familiarize children with a new group of words that have been placed on the Word Wall.

MATERIALS
- Word Wall containing high-frequency words
- Individual chalkboards or paper for each child

PROCEDURE

1. Select six high-frequency words and place them on the Word Wall.

2. Introduce the words to the children, one at a time, using the following format:

   - Point to a word and say it distinctly.

   - Have the children repeat the word after you.

   - Spell the word for the children as you clap each letter.

   - Have the children clap for each letter as they chant the letter aloud.

   - Have the children write the word on their individual chalkboards or paper. Check.

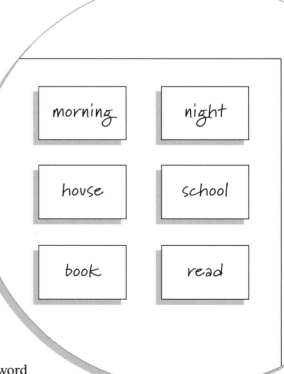

3. Tell the children they now are going to be "word detectives." Invite them to find one of the six words based upon the clues you give them and write on their chalkboards. Offer clues such as the following:

   - The word begins with /b/ and rhymes with *took*.

   - The word ends like *bead* and has four letters.

Continued.

- The word begins like *skate* and rhymes with *cool*.
- The middle of the word sounds like *loud* or *sound*.

4. To check the answer, say the clue word and let the children say the word they wrote and chant its spelling.

ASSESSMENT   Check answers on the individual chalkboards. Make anecdotal notes on difficulties with beginning sounds, ending sounds, vowel sounds, and finding rhyming words.

Notes for next time . . .

_____

_____

_____

_____

_____

_____

_____

_____

_____

_____

_____

_____

_____

_____

Building Words

SUGGESTED
GRADE LEVEL   *1*

PURPOSE   This hands-on activity helps children learn to look for the patterns in words, using individual letters—a useful decoding and spelling skill. Through active manipulation, they learn that changing just one letter or the location of a letter can change the whole word.

MATERIALS
- Letter tiles (commercial or made from file folders in 1-inch × 2-inch rectangles, enough sets for each child in the class)
- Letter holders (commercial or from Scrabble game)
- Plastic zippered bags for each set of letters
- Pocket chart and letter cards

PROCEDURE

1. In the pocket chart, display the letters *b, s, r, t, a,* and *i.* Ask the children to find these letters in their bag.

2. Say to the children, "Take two letters and make the word *at.* Put the word in your letter holder."

3. Ask for a volunteer to make the word in the pocket chart using the letter cards. Have the children look at the word in the pocket chart and check their words. Say the word together slowly and chant the spelling, pointing to each letter as the children say the sound.

4. Tell the children, "Now I want you to build a different word with two letters by changing the first letter to an *i.*" Again, have a volunteer put the word in the pocket chart. Say the word *it* together and chant the spelling.

5. Say, "Now we are going to build a three-letter word by adding just one letter to the word *it.* Does anyone know what letter we can add to the word *it* to make *bit?*" The child with the correct answer goes to the pocket chart and makes the word with the letter cards as the other children make theirs from their letter tiles, placing them in their letter holders. They say the new word together and chant the spelling.

Continued.

6. Continue in this manner, adding and changing one letter at a time until the class has made the following words: *sit, sat, rat, bat.*

7. In subsequent sessions, use different letter combinations, generally including four consonants and two vowels to build new words. Add these words to a Word Wall for later reinforcement.

ASSESSMENT   By observing the letter holders of individual children, you can determine who has trouble manipulating letters to build words and which letters are causing the problems, for individual interventions.

Notes for next time . . .

_____

_____

_____

_____

_____

_____

_____

_____

_____

_____

_____

_____

_____

Silly Food Rhymes

SUGGESTED GRADE LEVEL   *K–1*

PURPOSE   This activity uses food rhymes such as "feetloaf" for "meatloaf," which children find hilarious. Besides participating in an enjoyable listening activity using a wonderful selection from children's literature, the children will gain practice in manipulating beginning sounds themselves to create silly nonsense words that rhyme with their favorite foods.

MATERIALS
- *The Hungry Thing,* by Jan Slepian (1976)
- Chalkboard or overhead projector and transparency

meeza	=	pizza
blacos	=	tacos
rot hogs	=	hot dogs
bamburgers	=	hamburgers
mice scream	=	ice cream
falana	=	banana
ballad	=	salad
snake	=	cake

PROCEDURE

1. Read the children the book *The Hungry Thing.* To reinforce the concept of rhyme, stop when you get to the rhyming part of each phrase and allow the children to shout out the predictable rhyme. For example:

   "I know for sure," said a lady in red,
   "It's a cute little baby that stands on her [head]."

2. After reading the book and discussing it with the children, read it again, this time asking the children to name some of the foods rhymed in the book. Write the words on the board as the children say them.

3. Explain to the children that they now are going to make up some rhymes for their favorite foods. Ask the children to raise their hand when they can think of a food that was not mentioned in the story.

4. Write on the board or overhead transparency, the foods that the children suggest, sounding them out in front of the children.

5. For each food the children suggest, ask them to substitute the first sound with a different sound that provides a rhyme. Example: *hot dog* might become *rot hog.* Follow this procedure for all of the foods the children suggest.

6. Reread the book using the new foods and rhymes the children suggest.

ASSESSMENT   Ask each child to write down on a piece of paper three new foods and corresponding rhymes that were not listed on the board.

Notes for next time . . .

_____

_____

_____

_____

_____

_____

_____

_____

_____

_____

_____

_____

_____

_____

_____

_____

Lonely Letter Poem

(Adapted from For the Love of Language, *by Cecil)*

5

**SUGGESTED
GRADE LEVEL** *K–3*

PURPOSE   Through the use of alliteration in a poetic format, children can think of many words beginning with the same sound to tell about a topic, thereby experimenting with sound/letter relationships and expanding their vocabulary at the same time.

MATERIALS
- Overhead projector and transparency
- Dry-erase pen

PROCEDURE

1. Write the following poem on an overhead projector transparency and read it to the children, exaggerating the /t/ sounds in the words:

   Turtles

   Turtles are tame,
   Turtles are timid.
   Ticklish, tiny
   Tender, tasty.
   Terrible, tacky,
   Teeny, tan.
   Turtles are timid,
   Turtles are tame.

Dogs

Dogs are dirty,
Dogs are dear.
Dusty, dingy,
Daring, dark.
Delightful, dreamy,
Ditzy, dry.

Dogs are dear,
Dogs are dirty.

2. Ask the children what they notice about the poem, guiding them to see that all the adjectives describing "turtle" begin with the same letter. Select a plural noun (such as *foods, pets, mothers, dogs, toys, cookies*). Write the word on the overhead projector transparency, segmenting the sounds for the children. Explain that they will be writing a poem about this topic.

3. Ask the children to tell you the first letter and sound in the word.

4. Invite the children to brainstorm some words that tell about, or describe, the topic. For *foods*, for example, the children might brainstorm the words *fine, fantastic, funny, fattening, fast, famous, fabulous, filling,* and *fussy.*

Continued.

5. Using the brainstormed words, have the children help you write a new poem about their topic in the same format as in the turtle poem. Their poem might turn out to be, for example:

> Foods
>
> Foods are fattening,
> Foods are filling.
> > Fantastic, fine,
> > Fabulous, fast.
> > Famous, fussy,
> > Funny, familiar.
> Foods are filling,
> Foods are fattening.

6. Read the poem chorally several times with the children, inviting them to exaggerate the /f/ sounds.

7. Place the brainstormed words on a Word Wall.

8. Run off copies of the poem, leaving space at the bottom for each child to illustrate his or her class poem. Encourage the children to take their poems home to read to their families.

ASSESSMENT Have each child read his or her poem aloud to you, and offer assistance as necessary. Note, in particular, any inaccuracies with the targeted letter/sound.

Notes for next time . . .

_____

_____

_____

_____

_____

Eat Your Vowels

SUGGESTED
GRADE LEVEL *K–1*

PURPOSE Short vowels are often the most difficult for children to hear and remember. This activity provides a concrete frame of reference for all the short vowels, making them easier to remember, especially for children for whom English is a second language.

MATERIALS
- Red Jell-o in small plastic cups, enough for every child
- Enough 1-inch Gummi insects for all children
- Apples, cut in half and cored, enough for all in the class
- Lollipops for all children
- Bubble gum for each child

PROCEDURE

1. Write an upper-case and lower-case letter *e* on the chalkboard. Explain that the letter can have different sounds. One is the /ĕ/ sound in elephant (exaggerate the beginning sound of elephant). Have the children repeat the word after you.

2. Tell the children that they are going to eat a food that will help them remember this sound of /ĕ/. Pass out a cup of red Jell-o to each child. Have the children chant r–ĕ–d j–ĕ–ll–o, elongating the short /ĕ/ sound, three times.

3. Ask the children to brainstorm some other words that have this /ĕ/ sound in them. Write appropriate words on the chalkboard and, eventually, on a Word Wall.

4. Invite the children to eat the red Jell-o. Then ask them, "What did you just eat?" encouraging them to chant, "Red Jell-o!" three times. Finally, ask, "And what is the *e* sound in red Jell-o?" They should answer, "/ĕ/!" three times.

Eat Your Vowels

Continued.

5. Follow the same procedure for the remaining four vowel sounds, introducing, one at a time, "hălf an ăpple," "bŭbble gŭm," an "ĭnch of ĭnsect," and "lŏllipŏps."

ASSESSMENT   Using words on the class Word Walls as props, ask each child to say a word that contains each of the short vowels as you give them the target food prompt. For example, you might say "red Jell-o" and the child might respond, "gĕt" or "pĕppermint."

Notes for next time . . .

_____

_____

_____

_____

_____

_____

_____

_____

_____

_____

_____

_____

_____

_____

_____

_____

Phonogram Fun

**SUGGESTED
GRADE LEVEL**   *1–2*

PURPOSE   Children can demonstrate their understanding of phonograms, common ending patterns, by creating new words with the same ending through the enjoyable vehicle of a Dr. Seuss book, *The Sneetches*.

MATERIALS
- *The Sneetches* by Dr. Seuss
- Cards with phonograms on them
- Tokens or markers

PROCEDURE

"Sneetches!"

1. Review the concept of rhyme with the children by inviting them to participate in rhyming the following words: ball (call, fall, mall); can (tan, man, Dan, ran), etc.

2. Read the children the book *The Sneetches*. Read the book again, this time telling the children to listen for rhyming words as you read.

3. Pass out to each child three words containing phonograms, such as sock, clock, and rock. Tell the children the words on the cards are words they heard in the story.

4. Ask the children to read their cards to their neighbor and then use each word in a sentence. (If a child has difficulty with a word, the partner may help them, or they may look at the page in the book and use the context of the pictures to decide what the word is.)

5. Read the story one more time, asking the children to put a token on their words when they hear them in the story.

6. Instruct the children that the first child to have all three words covered is to say, "Sneetches!"

Phonogram Fun

Continued.

7. Ask the child to find each word on the page of the book where the word appears, point to the word, and say the word in the text that rhymes with it.

8. Write the rhyming words on a Word Wall and have the children identify the ending part that the two words have in common. Ask them if they can think of any more words that have the same ending (phonogram, or rime). Write them on the Word Wall.

9. Return to reading the book until another child calls out "Sneetches!" Continue the process until reaching the end of the book.

ASSESSMENT   Use anecdotal notes to record who was able to read the phonogram, who was able to create a sentence using the phonogram, and who contributed new rhyming words for the Word Wall.

Notes for next time . . .

_____

_____

_____

_____

_____

_____

_____

_____

_____

_____

_____

SUGGESTED GRADE LEVEL K–1

PURPOSE   Knowledge of the alphabet is essential to early literacy. This activity makes the transition, in an enjoyable way, from knowledge of the letters, in sequence, to an understanding of the sounds those letters make.

MATERIALS
- Alphabet cards
- Tape recorder
- Tape of marching music
- Large hat

PROCEDURE

1. Seat the children in a circle on the floor.

2. Using capital letters to begin, and then mixing in lower-case letters, put the alphabet letters in the hat and ask each child to take a turn at drawing a letter out of the hat.

3. Have the children identify the letter and then think of something that begins with the sound the letter makes. If children have problems, offer several examples of something that begins with the sound until they are able to make the connection between the letter and its corresponding sound.

4. When all the children have had a turn, ask them to place their letter on the floor to mark their place.

5. Play a march tune and have the children march quietly around the circle until the music stops.

6. When the music stops, tell the children to sit down by the new letter they are closest to. Have the children, one by one, identify their letters and think of a word beginning with the new letter.

7. Repeat the above procedure several times.

Variation

The activity can be done using words; the children then think of rimes or other words with the same beginning letter(s).

ASSESSMENT   Use the Knowledge of Sounds and Letters Checklist (*SAB,* p. 280) or use letter cards from this activity to assess each child individually on knowledge of the letters, sounds, and ability to produce a word with the sound.

Notes for next time . . .

_____

_____

_____

_____

_____

_____

_____

_____

_____

_____

_____

_____

Reread Alouds

**SUGGESTED
GRADE LEVEL** *1–3*

PURPOSE Current research suggests that children become more accurate and fluent when they read the same passage several times, and that their understanding of what they have read also increases. This activity will make repetition enjoyable for young children.

MATERIALS
- Tape recorder
- Blank tape
- Material of the child's choosing
- Simple bar graph to show progress
- Stopwatch or clock with second hand

PROCEDURE

1. Help the children each select a short passage that is a bit difficult for them (at their instructional level).

2. Have the children write down any words they cannot decode.

3. Have the children attempt to decode the problem words, then tell them the words. Record specific phonetic elements that are troublesome, and place in the child's file.

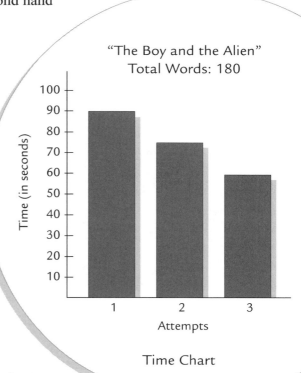

"The Boy and the Alien"
Total Words: 180

Time (in seconds)

Attempts

Time Chart

4. Ask the children individually to read the passage aloud as you tape-record it. Using a watch or clock with a second hand, record the time. Note any errors.

5. Tell the children that they are now going to beat their record by reading the same passage faster. Again, record the reading time for each child and note any errors. Repeat this process several times in a relaxed, gamelike fashion.

9 *Reread Alouds*

Continued.

6. Help the children use a bar graph to compare their reading time and their accuracy between the first and last readings. Discuss the children's growth individually with them.

ASSESSMENT   Photocopy the bar graph and place it in the child's file as an ongoing assessment of fluency and accuracy.

Notes for next time . . .

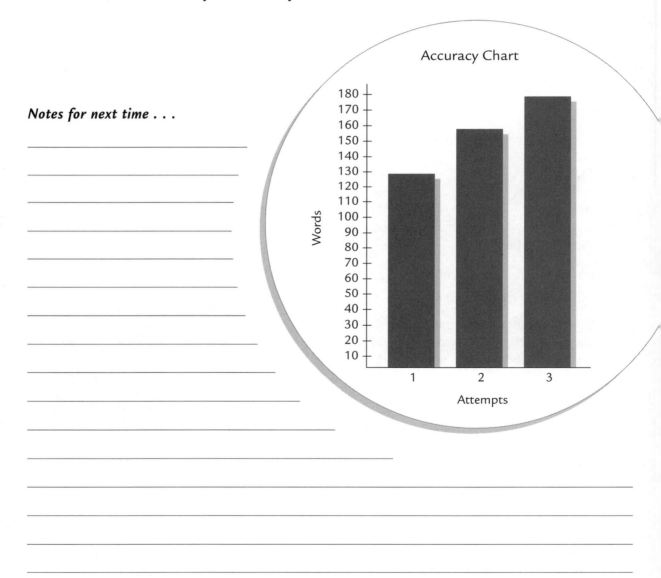

Venn Diagram Sort

SUGGESTED
GRADE LEVEL   *1–3*

PURPOSE   Word sorts help children to focus on conceptual and phonological attributes of
words and to identify recurring patterns. In this activity, pairs of children sort
words according to two different features, for example, differing vowel sounds
or common onsets or rimes.

MATERIALS   ● Chart paper
                 ● Markers

PROCEDURE

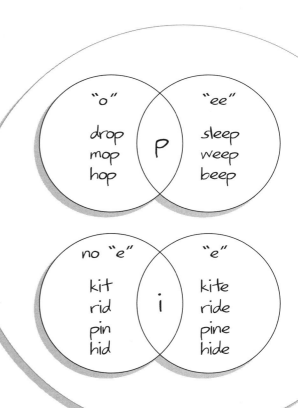

1. Compile two lists of three or four words
each that have sound and letter similarities as well as sound and letter
differences. For example, one list may
consist of *drop, mop,* and *hop* and the
other list might consist of *sleep,*
weep, and *beep.* (Although the
words in one list and the words in the
other list all end with the letter *p,* the
two lists have words with different
beginnings/onsets and different vowels.)

2. Write the words from Step 1 on the
board in no particular order. Say the words
and have the children repeat them after you.

3. Draw two overlapping circles on the chart paper.
Write a word from one list in one circle and a word
from the other list in the other circle.

4. Write the feature that the words from both lists have in common (the letter *p*) on the overlapping portion of the diagram.

5. Ask the children to select a word from the board and tell on which circle it should go and
why. Invite them to write the word on the appropriate circle (see illustration).

6. Repeat this procedure with several other pairs of lists until the children are proficient at identifying the similarities and differences between two sets of words.

7. For a further challenge, provide pairs of children with Venn diagrams drawn on chart paper. Encourage the children to do their own Venn diagram sorts.

ASSESSMENT   Observe individual children as they place the words on the circles or overlapping portion of the diagram. Provide one-on-one assistance to children who seem to have difficulty detecting patterns in words.

Notes for next time . . .

_____

_____

_____

_____

_____

_____

_____

_____

_____

_____

_____

_____

_____

Other Ideas & Activities

● **BEACH BALL PHONICS**

With a laundry marker, print a consonant letter on each panel of a beach ball. Toss the ball to a child and have the child say a word beginning with the sound of the letter that his or her hand is touching or near.

● **PICTURE CARDS**

Use picture cards of animals, foods, or other familiar items to help children experiment with the sounds in language. Model some simple one-syllable words and have children practice saying, then writing, the words in two parts—onset and rime.

● **CONCENTRATION**

Play the familiar game Concentration. Make a set of word cards and have pairs of children find the pairs of words that have the same beginning or ending sound.

● **CARTOON WORDS**

With the children, brainstorm some of the sounds and nonsense words that cartoon characters say ("vroom!" "bam!" "aaaack!"). Have the children experiment with the sound/symbol relationship by helping you sound out these words as you print them on the board.

● **PINK PANSY PASS**

In this game, a paper or silk flower is passed from one child to the next, using the beginning sound of the flower to form a memory game. The first child holds the flower and says a word with the same beginning sound, writing the letter on the board. The next child must say that word and another word beginning with the same letter. The game ends when someone forgets an item.

● **MARY WORE HER RED DRESS**

Chant the phrase with the children: "Mary wore her red dress, red dress, red dress. Mary wore her red dress all day long." Ask the children to change the chant by adding a new piece of clothing that has an alliterative name. Examples: Gary wore his blue blazer; Jenny wore her pink poncho; Jose wore his purple pants.

● **RHYME LISTS**

On a piece of chart paper, write a favorite poem of the children. Read the poem chorally with the children and discuss the rhyming words. Invite the children to write these words on the chalkboard. Encourage them to think of other words that rhyme with words in the poem and write them on the board.

● **CRAYON WORDS**

With a crayon, write several simple words on a large sheet of tagboard. In front of the children, trace the letters with your finger as you blend one sound with another (e.g., mmmmaaaannnn).

Ask the children to write the same word with crayons in large letters on their own paper and practice blending the sounds while tracing each letter with their finger.*

- **HOLIDAY WORDS**
  During holiday seasons, brainstorm with the children words that are associated with the season and create a Word Wall using these words. Ask the children to circle the words that have the same beginning or ending sound.

- **FLOWER POWER**
  Depending upon what you wish to emphasize, select a specific onset or rime and write it on the board. Give a sheet of colored construction paper to each child and have him or her cut out flower shapes. On these shapes ask them to write a word that has the same onset or rime. Tape the ends of these shapes into a circle. When several circles have been constructed with differing onsets or rimes, you have a brightly colored flower bulletin board.

- **BRICK HOUSES**
  Make a brick house on the board by drawing a rectangle on the bottom of the board and writing within it a word that contains a phonological element you have introduced (for example, the *spr* blend). Tell the children they will help to build a house by adding bricks with words that begin with the same three letters. Make a rectangle beside or above yours and invite a volunteer to write a word beginning with *spr* on the brick. Repeat until you run out of words.

- **SOUND SEARCH**
  Encourage the children to look through books they are reading to find words that have the same letters or sounds as the one you are studying—for example, /oo/. Make a list of these words and create a Word Wall from them.

- **CLOTHESLINE**
  Hang a clothesline across a section of your classroom. Write a word on the chalkboard, such as the word *moon*. Give the children 3" × 5" cards. As the children think of words that contain the same sound symbol (soon, toot, poodle), have them write the word on their card, say it for the class, and pin the word on the clothesline with a clothespin.

* This activity has extra tactile/kinesthetic benefits.

Koch, Michelle. *Hoot Howl Hiss.* (New York: Greenwillow, 1991).

Words and illustrations depicting sounds that animals make. Decoding skills are utilized as young readers decipher captions that go with the illustrations.

Raffi. *Down By the Bay.* (New York: Crown, 1987).

A song celebrating silly rhymes: "Did you ever see a whale with a polka-dot tail, Down by the bay?" Lends itself to choral reading or singing. Reinforces rhyme and long /a/ and long /o/ patterns. Part of Raffi *Songs to Read* series.

Salisbury, Kent. *A Bear Ate My Pear.* (New York: McClanahan, 1998).

A phonics pop-up book using beautiful illustrations and word families. Gives examples of short vowels, the silent /e/, two vowels together, and some consonants and blends. These phonics elements can be used for reinforcement after direct teaching.

Serfozo, Mary. *Joe Joe.* (New York: Simon & Schuster, 1993).

Features Joe Joe, a small boy, who bangs a stick on a fence, bongs a garbage can, splashes, stops, claps, squishes, slips, and drips. Reinforces consonant clusters.

Snow, Pegeen. *Eat Your Peas, Louise.* (Chicago: Children's Press, 1993).

A story about a parent pleading with a reluctant Louise to eat her peas. Nothing works—neither threats nor bribery—until he says, "Please." Reinforces long /e/ patterns.

Vaughn, Marcia. *Hands Hands Hands.* Reading, PA: Mondo, 1995).

Pictures children showing what they can do with their hands: tug, hug, tickle tiny toes, plant, pick, and so forth. Reinforces long /e/ and short vowel patterns.

Other Resources for Teaching Phonics

For the Love of Language: Poetry Scaffolds for Every Learner, by Nancy Lee Cecil (Winnipeg, Manitoba: Peguis Publishers, 1994).

Ideas to help children explore many types of poetry. Each poetry activity includes a description, an easy-to-follow pattern, and a lead-in activity to help motivate children and help the teacher prepare for the session. Also includes samples of poetry written by children.

Phonics from A to Z: A Practical Guide, by Wiley Blevins (Jefferson City, MO: Scholastic Professional Books, 1998).

An essential resource providing teachers with a balanced look at how to incorporate a phonics program into reading instruction.

Phonics That Work! New Strategies for the Reading/Writing Classroom, by Janiel Wagstaff (Jefferson City, MO: Scholastic Professional Resources, 1998).

A detailed, replicable description of how the author's integrated phonics program works in her second-grade classroom, including strategies, specific activities, and a minute-by-minute daily schedule.

Phonics, Too! How to Teach Skills in a Balanced Literacy Program, by Jan Wells and Linda Hart-Hewins (York, ME: Stenhouse Publishers, 1994).

From consonant blends and lists of high-frequency words to sentence structure, all the background teachers need to make skills a part of a strong literacy program.

Teaching Phonics Today: A Primer for Educators, by Dorothy S. Strickland. (Newark, DE: IRA, 1998).

Discusses ways in which reading instruction, particularly the teaching of phonics, has changed in recent years, and provides suggestions for helping children to use phonics as a key component of their overall reading development.

Whole-to-Part Phonics: How Children Learn to Read and Spell, by Henrietta Dombey, Margaret Moustafa, and the staff of the Centre for Language in Primary Education (Westport, CT: Heinemann, 1997).

A set of detailed, practical suggestions for promoting the knowledge children need to learn letter-sound relationships while focusing on construction of meaning in both reading and writing.

Word Matters: Teaching Phonics in the Reading/Writing Classroom, by Gay Su Pinnell and Irene Fountas (Portsmouth, NH: Heinemann, 1998).

A myriad of authentic and enjoyable activities to engage young children with the kind of personally satisfying word study that will lead to prolific readers and writers.

In Closing

1. After using the activities in this section, what insights have you gained about how children develop understandings about how sounds and letters correspond? What did you discover about yourself as a teacher of phonics by teaching these activities?

2. Which activity did you think was most effective in developing each of the following phonic understandings? Why?

   ● Phonemic awareness

   ● Identification of letters

   ● The relationship between beginning sounds and letters

   ● The relationship between ending sounds and letters

   ● The memorization of high-frequency words

   ● Blending of sounds into words

3. Choose an activity that was easy and one that was difficult for the children with whom you worked. What about the activity made it easy/difficult? What adaptations, if any, would you make the next time you teach this lesson? How do you think these adaptations would make the activity more accessible for your learners?

4. What did you discover about the need to determine what children already know about a specific phonic element before beginning an instructional activity to teach phonics? How did the assessment suggestions at the end of each activity provide you with insights into the strengths and limitations of your teaching of phonics?

5. Select an activity that offered you the most insight into the phonics background of your learners. What did you discover? Cite examples of specific children with whom you worked.

6. Several of the activities asked you to have the children look for patterns in words and group them according to the patterns they discovered. What do these activities teach children about a strategy to decode unknown words?

7. Some of the activities had, as a major component, much reinforcement of phonemic awareness. Why would it be important to continue this instruction when children are already able to identify letters and sound out words?

8. Several activities asked you to place high-frequency words on Word Walls. What do you see as the advantages and disadvantages of using Word Walls? Do you think the introduction of high-frequency vocabulary is compatible with phonics instruction? Why or why not?

9. Children from other language groups often have a difficult time hearing and articulating certain sounds in the English language. Analyze three of the activities that ask children to use specific sounds that may be difficult for some children. How can each of these activities be made more accessible to ELL children?

10. Identify a child who does especially well during phonics instruction activities. What are the characteristics of this child? What additional activities might you include to assure that this child is appropriately challenged in future phonics instruction activities?

4
ACTIVITIES FOR SPELLING THROUGH EXPERIMENTING WITH PRINT

Introduction

Because spelling is one of the most visible manifestations of literacy, it holds an exalted place in our society. Therefore, teachers must understand the nature and function of spelling, or "sound mapping," and communicate to parents about how spelling proficiency actually evolves.

After many years of studying spelling, researchers have decided that spelling involves much more than simply memorizing the sequence of letters in a list of words. Just as the errors young children make in speaking or drawing get corrected after much practice, spelling will evolve after some direct instruction in how English orthography works. Spelling seems to develop in a fairly consistent and predictable way in all children, similar to the stages children pass through as they learn to speak. Knowing a bit about how this important literacy convention progresses will ease the anxiety that parents and others often have that the errors in early written work will become permanent.

J. Richard Gentry has analyzed the way in which children learn to spell and has identified five discrete stages that children go through.

1. The *precommunicative stage,* in which children are using strings of letters and other various symbols but have little or no idea which symbol stands for which sound.

2. The *semiphonetic stage,* wherein they realize a rudimentary relationship between sounds and letters but often use one letter to represent an entire word.

3. The *phonetic stage,* in which spellers tend to segment sounds according to what they hear.

4. The *transitional stage,* which finds children using rules and orthographic patterns they have been taught, and also becoming much more aware of the visual aspects of words.

5. The *correct, or conventional, stage,* when children have mastered many of the more sophisticated rules of orthography and also have acquired a large body of grade-appropriate words that they can spell correctly in their written work.

The following activities have been chosen because they allow young children to focus on the rules of English orthography and experiment with print in an enjoyable way. They are designed not to replace but, instead, to supplement a program of direct instruction in spelling.

Puzzlers

SUGGESTED
GRADE LEVEL   *K–1*

PURPOSE   Spelling riddles, such as the ones suggested here, combine foundational elements of phonemic awareness, such as the manipulation of sounds and sound segmentation, with deliberate mapping of the sounds using letters, or spelling. Because the riddles are oral, children must use their visual memory to think about the sounds and the letters.

MATERIALS   ● 5" × 8" word cards, one for each of the words used

PROCEDURE

1. Tell the children you are going to play a riddle game with them. You will ask them a question about some words and the sounds within them, and they are to guess the answer.

2. Model the game, by saying: In this game, I might say three words— *bunny, bat,* and *bean.* Then I would ask you, "Which letter is in all three words?" You would say "b." Or I might say, "I am in *top* but not in *hop.* What letter am I? I'm the letter *t."*

3. Begin with easier to hear questions containing only beginning sounds. Use the following riddles or add to them with your own:

> I am in tin, tomato, and tiny. What am I?
> I am in bag, bone, and bottle. What am I?
> I am in sun, soft, and sad. What am I?
> I am in land, loaf, and luck. What am I?
>
> Harder: I am in truck, train, and trust. What am I?
> I am in call but I am not in ball. What am I?
> I am in sing but I am not in wing. What am I?

I am in tin, tomato, and tiny.

What am I?

I am in truck, train, and trust.

What am I?

I am in call but I am not in ball.

What am I?

I am in try but I am not in sky.

What am I?

I am in time but I am not in lime. What am I?

I am in boy but I am not in toy. What am I?

Harder: I am in try but I am not in sky. What am I?

4. After each riddle has been discussed and answered orally, reinforce sound/symbol relationships by showing the word cards and pointing to the letters that are the same or were being manipulated.

5. For a greater challenge for children who are more capable spellers, invite them to create their own puzzlers to share with the rest of the class.

ASSESSMENT The riddles created for this activity can be used to assess either phonemic awareness or sound mapping ability by using the cards in two different ways.

1. Ask individual children who are not yet able to work with letters to tell only the sound represented by the words in the riddles (e.g., tin, tomato, and tiny all begin with the /t/ sound).

2. For children who are already working successfully with phonics, use the cards with individual students to ascertain which letters they are able to recognize, segment, and manipulate, and which letters require more work.

Notes for next time . . .

_____

_____

_____

_____

_____

_____

Guess and Spell

**SUGGESTED
GRADE LEVEL**   *2–3*

PURPOSE   The visual memory necessary for proficient spelling is highlighted in this activity, which asks children to spell the names of common objects in the classroom. The leader, a good speller whose prowess is highlighted, puts letters on the board as other students suggest them, allowing individual students to practice sound mapping in an enjoyable and nonthreatening gamelike activity.

MATERIALS   • Chalkboard

PROCEDURE

1. Select a proficient speller to be "it." This child selects a common object in the room and whispers its name to the teacher.

2. The other children in the class raise their hands, and the leader calls on them to guess the first letter of the chosen object. As they guess the correct letters, the leader puts them on the chalkboard.

3. When the first letter is guessed, the children start trying to guess the second letter, then the third letter, and so forth, until the entire word is spelled.

4. When any student thinks he or she can spell the total word after only a few letters have been guessed, that student may challenge the leader by spelling the complete word. If the word is spelled correctly, that student becomes "it."

ASSESSMENT Make a list of the words the leaders chose and use these as a spelling list for the week. In small groups, children can sort these words according to beginning or ending sounds, affixes, or other attributes. Make notes on children's strengths and needs observed through these activities.

Notes for next time . . .

_____

_____

_____

_____

_____

_____

_____

_____

_____

_____

_____

_____

_____

_____

_____

_____

_____

_____

Consonant Picture Match

SUGGESTED
GRADE LEVEL *K–1*

PURPOSE At the initial stages of spelling development, the children must begin to notice the visual differences in structure, as well as the sound differences, between letters that are dissimilar. This activity affords children enjoyable practice in discriminating between two letter sounds at a time.

MATERIALS
- Consonant picture cards
- Consonant letter cards

PROCEDURE

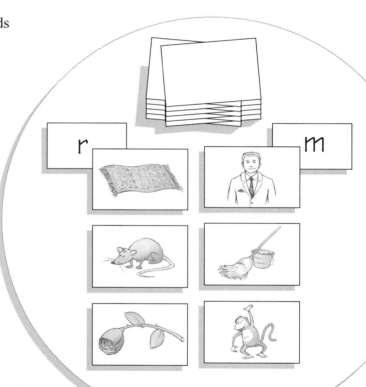

1. Begin with two letter sounds that are most dissimilar (e.g., r and m).

2. Choose two pictures, one each for the beginning sound corresponding to the two letters.

3. On a table or desk, place the pictures (e.g., rug and man) under the corresponding letter. Shuffle the remaining cards and say to the children: Now we are going to listen for the sounds at the beginning of these pictures. We will decide if the word begins like "rug" or like "man."

4. Model how you decide how the beginning sound is categorized by doing several in front of children until they have the idea. For example, if the picture is of a mouse, say: Mouse: mmmmmouse begins like mmmman, so I'll put it under the letter "m."

5. Invite the children to take turns deciding whether a picture belongs under the "r" or the "m" by sounding out the picture's beginning sound, as you did.

6. After all the pictures have been sorted in this manner, have the children help you name all the pictures in each category from the top down, exaggerating the beginning sound of each.

3 Consonant Picture Match

Continued.

ASSESSMENT Have individual children complete the sort while naming the picture and matching the letter with which it corresponds. Using a checklist, determine which children are able to complete this task and which children need further instruction in discriminating the targeted initial consonants.

Notes for next time . . .

Roots and Branches

**SUGGESTED
GRADE LEVEL**   *2–3*

PURPOSE   Children develop an understanding of the roots of words by seeing how the spelling of a word can change with the addition of suffixes. This activity can be adapted to any of the later spelling stages.

MATERIALS   ● Sets of four word cards for each of several regular root words and their common derivatives—for example:

march, marcher, marching, marched

fear, feared, fearful, fearing

dance, dancer, dancing, danced

call, called, calling, caller

play, player, playing, played

ask, asked, asking, asker

bake, baker, baking, baked

PROCEDURE

1. Make enough copies of each set of words to have four "books" (a "book" is all four cards with the same root) for each child. Divide the children into pairs.

2. Shuffle the cards and give six to each child.

3. Tell the children to sort their cards according to "roots," and give an example of how this would be done.

4. If a child holds four cards with the same root, that child has a "book" and lays down the cards on his or her desk.

5. At a given signal by the teacher, the children take turns asking their partner if they have a card with a certain root. Each child may continue asking for a card as long as the other child holds other words with the desired root.

6. Reverse the roles. The partner asks for root cards in a similar manner.

7. At the next signal, children select a different partner and repeat the procedure, laying down "books" as they are acquired.

8. A child wins the game when all of his or her cards are in "books."

Note: Care should be taken not to introduce elements for which the children are not developmentally ready—for example, doubling the final consonant of a root or completely changing the spelling, such as *teach* and *taught*.

ASSESSMENT Before the game, introduce the words to be assessed, and then use them for the weekly spelling lesson. When introducing more difficult stem changes, play the game again, incorporating the new spelling patterns.

Notes for next time . . .

_____

_____

_____

_____

_____

_____

_____

_____

_____

_____

_____

Smoked Bacon

SUGGESTED GRADE LEVEL *2–3*

PURPOSE   This activity forces children to attend to the exact sequence of letters that comprise words, to hold them in their visual memory, and then to actively form those words using their body as a "place holder."

MATERIALS

- Two sets of large cardboard letters, each set containing each of the letters in the words "smoked bacon"

PROCEDURE

1. Divide the class into two teams.

2. Have the teams stand up and face each other.

3. Distribute one letter card to each team member. Ask the children to hold their letter up prominently so the other team can clearly see it.

4. Call out an anagram, or a word that can be spelled with the letters from these two words (there are at least 100).

5. Ask the members of each team to rearrange themselves to form the letters in the word in order. The first team to get in the correct position gets 1 point. One child from the winning team is selected to write the new word on the chalkboard. The team with the most points wins the game.

ASSESSMENT   For the final weekly spelling test, use the anagrams from the words "smoked bacon." As a bonus, use two different words, such as baby sister, and ask the children to see how many new words they can create from these.

Notes for next time . . .

_____

_____

_____

_____

_____

_____

_____

_____

_____

_____

_____

_____

_____

_____

_____

_____

_____

_____

Flower Chains

SUGGESTED
GRADE LEVEL *2–3 (can be adapted to any grade level)*

PURPOSE This activity promotes interest in words, strengthens visual memory, and shows children how many words they are able to generate and spell. The integration with art makes this activity especially appealing.

MATERIALS
- Pencil
- Writing paper
- Colored construction paper
- Paste

PROCEDURE

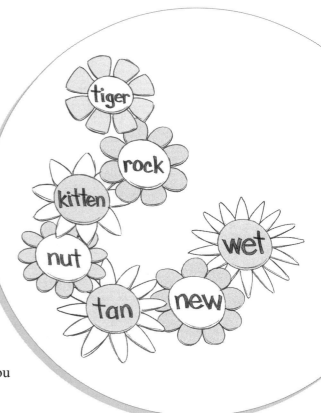

1. Cut out a series of flower shapes from colored construction paper. Put these aside.

2. Explain that you are going to see how many words you can make into a flower chain by saying a word, spelling it, and then thinking of a new word that begins with the last letter of the first word. For example, you might say: "My word is man, m-a-n. My next word is nut, n-u-t. My next word is tan, t-a-n, and so forth.

3. As you spell out the words, write them on the chalkboard, underlining the last letter of the first word, the first letter of the second word, and so forth. Keep adding words until all the children are able to tell you the letter the next word must start with.

4. Transfer the word list from the board to the flowers, one word per flower.

5. Paste the flowers together so corresponding beginning letters and ending letters follow one another.

Flower Chains

Continued.

6. Finally, connect the flowers when one word ending is the same as the first letter of the original word (see illustration).

7. Ask the children to write down a favorite word, perhaps from their weekly spelling list. Invite them to then write down as many words as they can think of using the first letter/last letter sequence. Encourage them to sound out unfamiliar words. Use these for future weekly spelling lists.

8. Pass out colored construction paper and have the children make flowers to correspond to their words. Help them to make flower chains by connecting the flowers where the first and last letters match.

ASSESSMENT   As the children are creating their lists, walk around the room taking anecdotal notes on each child's ability to sound out words, as well as the words memorized. Note which high-frequency words are generally giving the class problems. Include these in the weekly spelling list, or create a special Word Wall for them.

Notes for next time . . .

_____

_____

_____

_____

_____

_____

_____

_____

Memory Game

**SUGGESTED
GRADE LEVEL** *2–3*

PURPOSE   Besides improving visual memory and motivation for spelling new and familiar words, this activity stimulates the acquisition of new meaning vocabulary for English language learners.

MATERIALS
- Picture cards for 10 to 15 objects
- Objects (marble, pencil, scissors, paperclip, ruler, yo-yo, stamp, tack, book, etc.)
- Pencils and paper

PROCEDURE

1. Put the children in groups of three.

2. Tell the children that you are going to show them some pictures, and later some objects, and that they are to study these carefully and try to remember each one.

3. Show the pictures to the children, one at a time. Clearly state the name of each object for the benefit of ELL children.

4. Conceal the pictures. Ask the children to write down the names of every one they can remember.

5. When the children have remembered all they can, allow them to consult with their other two group members to see if they recall these pictures and to check on the correct spelling. Have the groups form a new, corrected list with as many words as each group can remember.

6. Bring out the objects. Have members from each group take turns writing the name of an object on the chalkboard.

7. Create a Word Wall with these words.

ASSESSMENT   Collect the lists of initial spelling attempts from individual children before they receive input from their group. Analyze the spelling patterns of the children individually according to their stage of spelling development. Consider homogeneous regrouping according to the children's individual stage of spelling development.

Notes for next time . . .

_____

_____

_____

_____

_____

_____

_____

_____

_____

_____

_____

_____

_____

_____

_____

_____

_____

Rhyming Race

SPELLING THROUGH EXPERIMENTING WITH PRINT

SUGGESTED GRADE LEVEL *1–2*

PURPOSE
This activity gives young children practice in recognizing the patterns of rimes, or phonograms, in the English language, introduces the concept of homophones, and offers a welcome variation from the routine weekly spelling test.

MATERIALS
- Pencils
- Paper
- List of spelling words that have common rimes (e.g., call, sand, date, fold, fill, ran, pin, teach, grew, like)

PROCEDURE

1. Review the concept of rhyming with the children. Guide them to see that words that have the same ending sounds have rimes that are often spelled the same way. Offer examples such as the words *man* and *tan*. Invite the children to add new beginning letters to these words as you write them on the board or on a Word Wall.

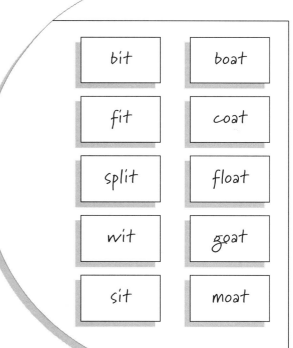

2. Say the first spelling word (e.g., grew). Ask the children to write it on their papers.

3. Ask for a volunteer to write the spelling word on the board so all the children may see if their word was spelled correctly.

4. Invite the children to write down as many rhyming words as they can for the word on the board (for the word *blew:* flew, drew, few, stew, knew, crew, chew, threw).

5. Discuss words that sound the same but are spelled differently than the original word (for example: blew, blue; through, threw; see, sea). Introduce the concept of homophones (also called homonyms) for these word pairs.

6. Write the sets of rhyming words on a Word Wall, where they can be used for original poetry. Create a separate column for words that sound the same as the original word but are spelled differently (homophones).

ASSESSMENT   Invite the children to create original rhymes using the rhyming words on the Word Wall. Note how each child is able to use rhyming patterns and decide when a word is a homophone.

Notes for next time . . .

_____

_____

_____

_____

_____

_____

_____

_____

_____

_____

_____

_____

_____

_____

_____

Spelling Tic-Tac-Toe

**SUGGESTED
GRADE LEVEL**   *2–3*

PURPOSE   This activity can be used to have the children focus on specific features in words, such as word beginnings, word endings, prefixes, roots, and suffixes, when children are in the transitional stage of spelling development.

MATERIALS
- Individual chalkboards or regular chalkboard
- Optional: Cardboard with a predrawn tic-tac-toe crosshatch (enough for each child)
- List of weekly spelling words, or other word list

PROCEDURE

1. Pair the children. Identify one child in each pair as player number one, and designate the other player as player number two.

2. Provide each pair with chalkboard space with a tic-tac-toe crosshatch, or an individual chalkboard with the crosshatch, or a specially made cardboard tic-tac-toe square.

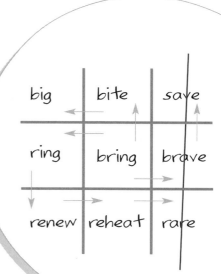

3. On the chalkboard or overhead projector transparency, write the spelling words from the weekly spelling list, a list of frequently missed words, or common "demons."

4. Ask player number one to place the first word from the list on any one of the nine spaces in the tic-tac-toe area—for example, the word *bring*.

5. Ask player number two to select a spelling word that has a common element—the same beginning, ending, prefix, suffix, or root—and place it in a position to block the first word, explaining to player number one what the two words have in common. For example, the child might select the word *ring*, explaining that both words have the same endings.

6. Have player number one select another word from the list that has an element in common with the word it will be next to, put it on the board to block, and state what the two adjoin-

ing words have in common. This player could select the word *renew,* as it has the same first letter as the word *ring.* The next player then might use a word such as *reheat,* as it has the same prefix as *renew.*

7. The object of the game is to write three words in line or diagonally that all contain a common element. Note: Children may write a new word of their own instead of choosing from the list as long as the new word contains an element in common with the word they are blocking.

Variation:

For children in earlier stages of spelling development, letters may be passed out and the children asked to simply spell three-letter words they make by the line or diagonally by connecting adjacent letters.

ASSESSMENT   Create a new list of 20 words with an assortment of roots, prefixes, and suffixes. In pairs, have the children do a closed word sort, categorizing the words in terms of common prefixes, suffixes, or roots. Ask each member of the pair to explain how they sorted the words.

Notes for next time . . .

_____

_____

_____

_____

_____

_____

_____

_____

Favorite Words

SPELLING THROUGH EXPERIMENTING WITH PRINT

SUGGESTED GRADE LEVEL   *1–3*

PURPOSE   Children learn to spell words more easily if they have special meaning for the children. In this activity, which can supplement the weekly spelling list or be used to supplant it for individual children who are struggling, children select their own words to learn to spell.

MATERIALS
- Word cards
- Crayons
- Metal notebook rings

PROCEDURE

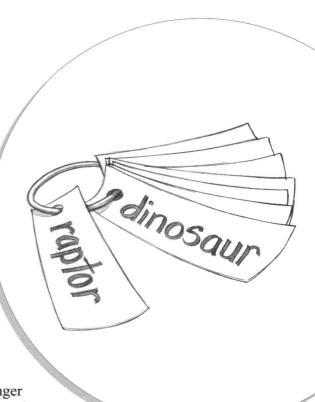

1. Individually, take children aside and ask them to think of a word they would like to learn how to spell (often, it is helpful to start with their name).

2. Write their word on a word card with the crayon.

3. Ask the child to tell you a short sentence that contains the word.

4. Write the child's sentence on the back of the word card, underlining his or her word.

5. Have the child read the word and the sentence on the back of the word card.

6. Ask the child to trace the word with a finger while saying each letter aloud, and then spell the word to you without looking at it.

7. Punch a hole in the word card and put it on a metal ring.

8. Add more words as each child is ready.

ASSESSMENT   Periodically have each child read the words and sentences. Then ask the child to spell the words either orally or on paper.

Notes for next time . . .

_____

_____

_____

_____

_____

_____

_____

_____

_____

_____

_____

_____

_____

_____

_____

_____

_____

Other Ideas & Activities

- **CHALKBOARD SPELLING**
Have children with fine-motor coordination problems write spelling words on the chalkboard with paint brushes and water.

- **MNEMONIC DEVICES**
Use mnemonic devices to help children remember difficult words by making specific associations with the word. Examples: *All right* is like *all wrong*. I want a *pie*ce of *pie*. A fri*end* is with you 'til the *end*.

- **ALLITERATIVE SENTENCES**
In small groups, have the children produce sentences all beginning with the same first letter. Examples: Does David dig for dusty dinosaurs? Freda fries frog fritters on Fridays.

- **TREASURE BOX**
Write the weekly spelling words on slips of paper, fold them, and put them into a "treasure box." Invite each child in turn to draw out a slip to be handed to you unopened. Pronounce the word and have the child attempt to spell it. Hand misspelled words to the child to study. Two children can provide extra practice for each other as they play this game quietly in a corner.

- **NOVELTY SPELLING**
Instead of calling words from a spelling list, say, for example, "Spell a word that rhymes with *joint*," "Spell a word that contains a *ph* that sounds like *f*," or "Spell a word that means _____ ."

- **BALLOONS**
Draw balloons on the chalkboard. Write the first letter of spelling words, one in each of the balloons. Each child who can say and spell the word that starts with a beginning letter "buys" a balloon. Let the child select the balloon he or she wants. If the child spells the word correctly, write the word and the child's name on the balloon.

- **PEAR TREES**
Divide the class into three committees to develop trees that "grow" pears with pairs of antonyms (big, little), homonyms (pair, pear), or synonyms (evil, bad). Put the pairs of words onto light green or yellow pears and add dark green leaves and brown branches for effect.

- **SPELLING JINGLES**
Establish spelling of new words by having the children compose jingles using the new word in a rhyme, thereby learning the new word and similar words as well. Example: When it is night, we need a light.

- **CROSSWORD PUZZLES**

  Make a crossword puzzle for the week's spelling words. For clues, use either the meaning or the word in context.

- **BEANBAG TOSS**

  Have a child stand in front of the room and toss a beanbag underhand to a seated child. As the beanbag is thrown, the child calls out a word that the catcher must spell. If the catcher spells the word correctly, it is that child's turn. A child may ask for help from a classmate.

- **SHAVING CREAM SPELLING**

  As a tactile activity, squirt some shaving cream on children's desks and ask them to write words using their fingers. When they are finished, they can wipe off the desks with paper towels, thereby cleaning the desks at the same time!

- **CONTRACTION HUNT**

  Have children look through newspapers and magazines for word pairs that can be changed into contractions, or contractions that can be changed into two separate words. Have children highlight these words and then place them on a word wall.

Children's Literature List

Brown, Craig. *City Sounds.* (New York: Greenwillow, 1992).

Depicts the sounds that Farmer Brown hears when he comes into the city to pick up some baby chicks. Reinforces long /e/ patterns as well as the use of phonics skills to decode city sounds.

Gardner, Beau. *"Have You Ever Seen . . ."? An ABC Book.* New York: BGA, 1986).

Asks questions that incorporate the sound correspondence being presented: "Have you ever seen a banana with buttons?" Reinforces beginning sounds and their spellings.

Raffi. *Spider on the Floor.* (New York: Crown, 1993).

A song telling about a spider that is on the floor and then crawls up the singer's leg, stomach, neck, face, and head. The book lends itself not only to choral reading and singing but also to recognizing the short /e/ pattern.

Roe, Eileen. *All I Am.* (New York: Bradbury Press, 1990).

A little boy telling about his unique qualities and interests: "I am a friend. I am an artist. I am a dancer." Provides a writing model and also reinforces the "er" suffix.

Wilson, Sarah, illustrated by Susan Meddaugh. *Good Zap, Little Grog.* (Boston: Candlewick, 1995).

The strange nonsense words and rhythmic patterns beg for repetition. Children will beg teachers to read the book again and again. The book can be used to create interest in words and encourage children to sound out or spell the nonsense words. After reading, children can be invited to tell other stories using made-up words.

Other Resources for Teaching Spelling

The Spelling Connection: Integrating Reading, Writing, and Spelling Instruction, by Ronald L. Cramer (New York: Guilford Publications, 1998).

Emphasizes practical classroom issues in exploring effective instructional strategies and their conceptual underpinnings; describes criteria for selecting spelling words; presents case studies showing the stages of spelling development; and addresses frequently asked questions about spelling.

Spelling Inquiry: How One Elementary School Caught the Mnemonic Plague, by Kelly Chandler and the Mapleton Teacher-Research Group (York, ME: Stenhouse Publishers, 1999).

A K–5 perspective on spelling development. Discusses how to foster inquiry-based learning about spelling and provides a detailed look at the workings of a schoolwide teacher-research group. Accessible and lively narrative blends the voices of a dozen of its members.

Spelling Instruction That Makes Sense, by Jo Phenix (Bothell, WA: Wright Group, 1998).

A refreshing book that explores when and how to introduce spelling in the classroom. Presents ways to capitalize on the "teachable moment" with individual students, small groups, and the whole class.

Spelling K–8: Planning and Teaching, by Diane Snowball and Faye Bolton (York, ME: Stenhouse Publishers, 1999).

Assists teachers in implementing specific types of spelling investigations, such as sounds and spelling patterns, by clearly outlining the general process involved in productive spelling explorations. Relates the teaching of spelling to reading and writing experiences in a variety of curriculum areas.

Spelling Strategies That Work: Practical Ways to Motivate Students to Become Successful Spellers, by Min Hong and Patsy Stafford (Jefferson City, MO: Scholastic Professional Resources, 1998).

Secrets of success in teaching spelling with an integrated language arts program written by seasoned classroom teachers. Documentation of how four primary students developed in spelling over a 2-year period illustrates the value of tailoring a program to individual needs.

The Spelling Teacher's Book of Lists, by Jo Phenix (Bothell, WA: Wright Group, 1998).

A collection of interesting words, spelling patterns, and facts designed for teachers who want to help children make sense of spelling. Lists focus on consonants, vowels, confusing spellings, linguistic roots, and useful rules.

The Violent E and Other Tricky Sounds: Learning to Spell from Kindergarten through Grade 6, by Margaret Hughes and Dennis Searle (York, ME: Stenhouse Publishers, 1997).

Uses detailed descriptions of growth in spelling by following children from kindergarten through grade 6. Reveals what children say and do as they come to understand spelling and its systematic nature.

Voices on Word Matters: Learning about Phonics and Spelling in the Literacy Classroom, edited by Irene C. Fountas and Gay Su Pinnell (Westport, CT: Heinemann, 1999).

An exploration, by experts in the field, of letter and word learning in a variety of reading, writing, and language contexts—with articles ranging from detailed observations of individual readers and writers to full-scale analyses of classroom processes and student work.

In Closing

1. After using the activities in this section, what insights have you gained into how children learn to spell? What did you discover about yourself as a teacher of spelling by teaching these activities?

2. Which of the following activities did you think were particularly effective for children at each of the following developmental spelling stages? Why?

   - The precommunicative stage

   - The prephonetic, or preliterate, stage

   - The phonetic, or letter name, stage

   - The transitional, or within-word, stage

   - The conventional, or syllable juncture, stage

3. What did you observe about the nature of children's "invented" or temporary spelling as a result of using the activities in this section?

4. What did you discover about the need to determine what children already know about the sound-symbol relationship before beginning a spelling lesson? How did the assessment suggestions at the end of each activity provide you with insights into the strengths and limitations of your teaching of spelling?

5. Select an activity that offered you the best insight into the developmental spelling stages of your learners. What did you discover? Cite examples of specific children with whom you worked.

6. Several of the activities offered a gamelike format. What do you see as the advantages and disadvantages of this format for spelling lessons?

7. One activity (*Favorite Words*) invited children to choose some of the words they would like to learn to spell. Do you think there were any motivational benefits to having the children do this? Describe your observations.

8. Some activities asked children to identify patterns or specific word parts such as roots. How do you think this strategy compares with having children memorize spelling rules and generalizations? Why?

9. Which activities were particularly difficult for your ELL children? What did you observe about their difficulties? How could you revise these activities to be more accessible to your ELL children?

10. Identify a child you think has a highly developed ability to spell unfamiliar words. What are the characteristics of that child? How did his or her behavior during the activities differ from that of other children? How will you adapt future spelling activities to assure that these children are appropriately challenged?

ACTIVITIES TO INCREASE VOCABULARY

Introduction

Learning the meanings of new words is without question crucial to a comprehensive literacy program for young learners. The more numerous the reading, writing, speaking, and listening activities, the more young children will come into contact with a variety of intriguing new words. These experiences help the vocabularies of children grow; and, through the excitement of reading and writing, these children also blossom into eager readers and writers.

Children add approximately 3,000 new words to their meaning vocabulary each year. This growth can be fostered through effective meaning vocabulary development activities such as helping children appreciate words, encouraging wide reading and application of new words, presenting strategies for figuring out new words, and the direct teaching of vocabulary and vocabulary-related skills. The ultimate goal of all vocabulary instruction should be to inspire children to become independent word collectors who actually enjoy encountering unfamiliar words. These children become those who comprehend best, and thus read the most, entering a self-perpetuating cycle of success.

The following activities are designed to foster a love for words, an appreciation for discerning just the right word when writing, and a better understanding of how words are formed in the English language. Many of the activities include pantomime or drawing to enhance the participation of English language learners.

Words in Color

1

SUGGESTED GRADE LEVEL *1–3*

PURPOSE
The definitions of words are remembered more easily when multisensory activities are used to focus children's attention on them. By sketching the meaning of a word, children are compelled to consider the context of that word; moreover, English language learners benefit from definitions, both by attempting to create the drawings themselves and by observing the drawings of their classmates. Articulating how the drawings fit the words provides an authentic purpose for critical thinking and oral language.

MATERIALS
- Colored marking pens
- White drawing paper
- Vocabulary words culled from text the children will soon read

PROCEDURE

1. To initiate this activity, demonstrate the end product by showing the children a drawing you have made that illustrates a word's meaning. Example: For the word "sad," draw a person frowning, perhaps near a dented car, or a rainy day, or a child with an ice cream cone with the ice cream on the ground.

2. Introduce each of the new vocabulary words, explaining the meaning of each. Ask several volunteers for different ways each word might be represented through a drawing.

3. Divide children into pairs. Distribute paper and pens and ask each group to discuss the meaning of each word and then agree upon an illustration for each word. The two children may choose to take turns drawing, or one may opt to simply offer suggestions.

4. As the children are discussing the words and the drawing, ask the groups to clarify the meanings of words about which they are unclear.

5. Have each pair select one of the words and explain to the rest of the class how their drawing illustrates the meaning of the word.

6. Taking each pair's favorite drawing, make a class book from the drawings, and title it "Words in Color."

ASSESSMENT Children's drawings, as well as their explanations of them, allow an important qualitative assessment of how well they understand the meanings of the new words. As a follow-up assessment, later ask individual children to define the words without the drawings, orally for preliterate children and in written form for older ones.

Notes for next time . . .

_____

_____

_____

_____

_____

_____

_____

_____

_____

_____

_____

_____

Teakettle

SUGGESTED GRADE LEVEL *2–3*

PURPOSE This activity shows children that many words are polysemantic—that they have multiple meanings—and therefore can be used in different ways.

MATERIALS
- Polysemantic words, each on a separate slip of paper (for example: ball, fast, change, rock, bank, miss, hand, sink, key)
- Box in which to put slips of paper

PROCEDURE

1. Use the word "ball" to explain to children that some words can have different meanings depending upon how they are used. Ask them to consider the following sentences as you write them on the board:

   > We had a *ball* at the party.
   > The princess danced all night at the *ball*.
   > The boy hit the *ball* with his bat.

2. Discuss how the word has different meanings in each sentence.

3. Explain that you are going to select a slip of paper from the box. On it will be a word that has several meanings. Make up a different sentence for each meaning, similar to the way you did with the word "ball." Instead of saying the word, however, say the word "teakettle." Offer the example:

   > The princess danced all night at the teakettle. Can you think of the word?
   > We had a teakettle at the party. Can you think of the word?
   > The boy hit the teakettle with his bat.
   > Now do you know the word?

4. Select another word from the box. Give children a sentence using one meaning of the word, then another, then another, always substituting the word "teakettle" for the word on the slip of paper.

5. Ask the children to raise their hand and guess as soon as they think they know the hidden word.

6. When the children seem to understand the concept of the game, invite them to select a word and make up sentences giving the different word meanings.

The boy moved *fast*.
The man held *fast* to his beliefs.
The family did not eat during the *fast*.

I got *change* from the five-dollar bill.
I had to *change* my clothes.
We had pudding for a *change*.

I didn't want to *rock* the boat.
I sat on the *rock* to think.
The boy enjoys *rock* music.

The teacher has the answer *key*.
I need a *key* to open the door.
Hard work is the *key* to success.

The boy sat on the river *bank*.
Don't *bank* on being home early.
I keep my money in a *bank*.

I *miss* my old friend.
I had to *miss* school when I was sick.
Miss Jones is a good teacher.

We washed our hands at the *sink*.
I watched the girl *sink* the basket.
I saw the boat *sink* in the water.

The audience gave the performer a *hand*.
I wear a ring on my right *hand*.
I will *hand* over my books.

Variation

Have the children draw an illustration for each meaning of each word.

Notes for next time . . .

_____

_____

_____

_____

_____

_____

Beef It Up

SUGGESTED GRADE LEVEL *2–3*

PURPOSE   With this activity, children can see how adding descriptive language and replacing "tired" words and phrases with more interesting vocabulary makes writing come to life. The activity is one of the few that also provides opportunities for group writing for young children, as well as an important experience in the evaluation of writing.

MATERIALS
- Simply written, short paragraph on an overhead transparency
- Overhead projector, blank transparency, and overhead writing utensil

PROCEDURE

1. Make a transparency of a simply written paragraph and put it on the overhead projector for children to see.

2. Read the paragraph aloud to the children as they follow along (for younger children, provide a hard copy and allow them to "track" as you read).

3. Ask the children if they think the first sentence could be improved by adding words, feelings, details, or by changing some "tired" words (such as "good," "happy," or "nice") without actually changing what the author was trying to say. Solicit some ideas from the children. Write the "improved" version of the sentence on a blank transparency.

4. Divide the class into groups of three. Assign one or two sentences from the paragraph to each group. Ask each group to "improve" their sentences by adding words, feelings, details, or by changing "tired" words.

5. When all the groups have finished editing, ask a child from each group to read his or her revised sentence. Write the revisions on the blank overhead transparency under the first sentence. Continue in this manner until the entire rewritten paragraph has been read.

6. Place the rewritten paragraph(s) alongside the original paragraph. Read the revised one first, then reread the original paragraph.

7. Ask the children to tell, in their own words, the difference between the two paragraphs. (The revised paragraph should appear more lively, descriptive, and interesting to the reader.)

8. Revisit this activity several times to ready the children to take part in a Writer's Workshop as helpful peer editors and self-evaluators.

3 Beef It Up

Continued.

Original paragraph:

Danny was a boy. He lived with his family in a small town. He always wanted to be in the circus. He thought it would be fun. One day he met a clown. The clown told him that living in a circus was hard work. You also have to travel from place to place. Danny changed his mind. Now he wants to be a fire fighter.

Revised paragraph(s):

Danny was a friendly eight-year-old boy with sandy brown hair and freckles. He lived with his mother and father and seven brothers and sisters on a small, tree-lined street in a little midwestern town. He dreamed of joining a circus in a far away city. "Becoming a circus performer seems like an exciting way to live," Danny blurted to his little sister.

One sunny afternoon Danny met a clown who was performing in a circus nearby. The clown, whose name was Bubbles, told Danny that becoming a circus performer took lots of difficult work. "A circus performer also has to travel from one location to another, all around the country," Bubbles whispered to Danny.

Danny thought about that for a while and finally decided not to join the circus after all. "I guess I will become a fire fighter just like my dad!" he exclaimed.

ASSESSMENT After implementing this activity several times, use the sample original paragraph in the illustration to see how well the children are able to revise the writing individually. Ask them to rewrite the paragraph, as they did in the activity, adding fresh words and phrases, dialogue, feelings, and other colorful details.

Notes for next time . . .

_____

_____

_____

Strange Expressions

SUGGESTED GRADE LEVEL   *2–3*

PURPOSE   Figures of speech, homophones, and other unusual expressions in the English language are often confusing for English language learners, as well as native English speakers. This activity focuses on some commonly used figures of speech through a whimsical text and invites children to collect others for group discussion.

MATERIALS
- *A Chocolate Moose for Dinner* by Fred Gwynne (New York: Simon & Schuster, 1976) or *The King Who Rained* by Fred Gwynne (New York: Simon & Schuster, 1974)
- Word Wall
- White drawing paper
- Marking pens

PROCEDURE

1. Read any of Fred Gwynne's books to the children. Each of these concerns a little girl trying to visualize the strange expressions her parents use, such as a "car pool," or a "king raining" or a "gorilla war."

2. Discuss the actual meaning of these expressions and their literal connotations.

3. Revisit the book, directing the children's attention to the illustrations, in which the little girl's literal interpretation of the terms leads to some hilarious visualizations.

4. With the children, brainstorm some other confusing expressions, idioms, or figures of speech that Gwynne's book did not cover, such as "She has a frog in her throat," or "I am tickled pink!" List these on chart paper, to which new expressions will be added over the next several weeks as they are encountered.

5. Encourage each child to select one of the expressions the class has collected and have each child illustrate the literal interpretation of the term and write the expression underneath.

6. Have each child share his or her illustration with the rest of the class, explaining what the expression actually means, yet what it sounds like it means to them.

7. Collate the pictures and bind them together into a class book entitled "Strange Expressions" or another title of the children's choice.

4 *Strange Expressions*

Continued.

I have a frog in my throat!

ASSESSMENT   Understanding of the these expressions can be determined by using the class book. Ask each child to read the expression (read the expression to preliterate children) and explain what each statement means and how each can be misinterpreted.

Notes for next time . . .

_____

_____

_____

_____

_____

_____

_____

Definitions

SUGGESTED
GRADE LEVEL   *1–3*

PURPOSE   This writing activity allows the children to use the poetic form of blank verse to define an entity by free-associating their personal feelings and reactions to it, and also considering what the entity is *not*.

MATERIALS
- Pencils
- Lined writing paper
- Sample poem written on an overhead transparency or chalkboard

PROCEDURE

1. Select a common state of being about which to brainstorm with the children. Examples: happiness, anger, jealousy, loneliness, confusion. (Younger children may be more comfortable using concrete entities such as lions, toys, friends, brothers, stars, or shoes.)

2. Stimulate thinking about the chosen word by asking questions such as, "What is it? What is it like? What is it not like? What are some examples of it?"

3. Have the children follow along as you read the sample poem or another of your choice, to inspire children and demonstrate the format.

4. Have the children select a topic, such as *puppies*. Write a group poem together on the chalkboard, with each line beginning with, "Puppies are . . ." and alternating lines beginning with "But puppies are not . . . ."

5. When the children have run out of ideas on the topic, read the poem together chorally, using a left-to-right motion to help children follow along.

Vacations

Vacations are fun and relaxing
But vacations are not being really
  bored.

Vacations are sleeping late
But vacations are not going to
  bed early.

Vacations are going to the lake
  or camping
But vacations are not staying
  home and doing nothing.

Vacations are fishing and hiking
But vacations are not cleaning
  up and doing chores.

Vacations are fun
But coming home to my pets is
  good, too!

6. Brainstorm some other ideas for topics that can be defined in this manner. Write them on the chalkboard and ask the children to select one.

7. Distribute the writing paper and ask each child to write a definition poem using the format of one line telling what the entity is and the next line telling what it is not. For younger children or children struggling with writing, provide sentence stems for each line ("Puppies are ___. But puppies are not ___"), allowing them to write as much or as little as they can.

8. Have the children illustrate their definition poems and read them aloud in small share groups.

ASSESSMENT   Examine the individual poems to determine if each child is able to use the contrasting format to define his or her chosen feeling or concrete entity.

Notes for next time . . .

_____

_____

_____

_____

_____

_____

_____

_____

_____

_____

Matrix

SUGGESTED
GRADE LEVEL   *2–3*

PURPOSE   Certain meaning vocabulary is easily forgotten because it pertains to a specific subject area and is not used in everyday conversation. To teach children domain-specific vocabulary, the following graphic is helpful and can lead to rich comparison-and-contrast discussion about the topic.

MATERIALS   • Chalkboard or overhead projector

PROCEDURE

1. A matrix, also called a Semantic Feature Analysis, can be used to discuss attributes of items in a specific class and to discriminate between them. Example: You are preparing to take the children to the zoo and you want to discuss some animals they will see.

2. Brainstorm with the children all the animals they might expect to see in the zoo. (For children who may lack background knowledge, provide picture books as aids.)

3. On the board or using an overhead projector transparency, write horizontally across the top of the board the names of animals the children have brainstormed, sounding out the spelling with the children.

	legs	fur	mane	hump	gills	lungs	tail	hooves	webbed feet	bill	trunk
monkey											
snake											
ostrich											
elephant											
camel											
panda											
lion											
shark											
duck											
polar bear											

4. In a vertical column to the left of the line of animals, create a list of attributes, or features, that animals could have. Define domain-specific vocabulary that might be unfamiliar to children, such as gills, mane, scales, hooves, webbed feet, bill, trunk, plumage, and hump.

5. Examine the cells one by one and, after you explain the attribute, ask the children to decide whether the animal in question possesses that feature. Write "yes" in the cell if the animal does and "no" if it does not. If the attribute is a quantifiable feature such as "legs," write the

number in the cell. Rich discussion can ensue when children try to determine, for example, if a snake has a tail or if an elephant has fur.

6. Have each child select an animal and write one or more expository sentences describing it, using information contained in the matrix.

Note: For English language learners or preliterate children, you may want to provide pictures of the animals and their attributes while retaining the same level of discussion and vocabulary development.

ASSESSMENT As the children are busy writing their sentences, use the time to do individual vocabulary assessments. Taking notes, ask the children to tell you everything they know about each of the animals as you mention their names one by one. Look for children to use the new vocabulary words.

Notes for next time . . .

_____

_____

_____

_____

_____

_____

_____

_____

_____

_____

Describe the Character

(Adapted from Schmidt, 1993)

7

SUGGESTED GRADE LEVEL *1–3*

PURPOSE   In this cooperative group activity, the children use oral language to discuss the outside features (appearance) and the inside features (feelings, personality, character) of major characters from stories they have just read.

MATERIALS
- 3" × 5" cards with the name of a literary character on each
- Book from which each character came
- Chart paper for each group
- Colored markers

PROCEDURE

1. Hold up the character cards, one at a time, for the entire class. Revisit their parts in stories that recently have been read.

2. Select one character, such as Amelia Bedelia, to use as a demonstration.

3. Make two columns on the chalkboard, one labeled "outside" and the other labeled "inside."

4. Ask the children to brainstorm the best words they can think of to first describe Amelia's outside, or her appearance. Write their suggestions under the "outside" column (e.g., thin, old-fashioned, dark-haired, grown-up). Do the same for their suggestions for Amelia's inside, or feelings and personality (e.g., confused, hard-working, funny, kind).

5. Place the children in small cooperative groups of three children each. Give one character card to each group.

Inside

confused
hard-working
funny
kind

Outside

thin
old-fashioned
dark-haired
grown-up

Describe the Character

Continued.

6. Invite the children to revisit their character in the story from which he or she came. Have them pay careful attention to the character's physical appearance and then, using colored markers, draw a picture of their character on the top of the chart paper.

7. Ask the groups to brainstorm as many words as they can think of for their literary character for both categories, inside features and outside features.

8. Have a member from each group share his or her chart with other members of the class, explaining their drawing, their word choices, and how they were selected.

ASSESSMENT   Circulate around to each of the cooperative groups and take notes on the nature of the discussions and number of different words that each child generates.

Notes for next time . . .

_____

_____

_____

_____

_____

_____

_____

_____

_____

_____

_____

_____

Peer Teaching

(Adapted from Blachowicz & Fisher, 1996)

SUGGESTED GRADE LEVEL *2–3*

PURPOSE Some researchers believe children can learn vocabulary best from other children because they are at the same cognitive level of operations. This activity allows children to teach words to each other, thereby benefiting from figuring out how to explain the word to another child.

MATERIALS
- Three index cards per child
- Writing utensils

PROCEDURE

1. Divide the children into groups of three. Give three index cards to each child in each group.

2. As the children are doing recreational reading, ask them to select one word they come across for which they do not know the meaning.

3. When the reading session is over, ask the children to prepare to discuss their word in a small group by writing the word and the sentence in which it appears on all three of the cards.

> EXHAUSTED
>
> "Jeremy was exhausted after completing the 10-mile hike in the Sierras."
>
> very tired

4. Invite the children to try to determine the meaning of the word by (a) using the context of the sentence, (b) asking a resource person to explain it, or (c) using the dictionary, for those who are able to do so.

5. Have the first child in each group pass out his or her cards to the other members of the group. Have that child begin by reading his or her word in the context of the sentence as the others follow along.

6. Ask the other two students to discuss the possible meaning of the word from the context. They decide the final meaning in collaboration with the child who brought the word to the group.

7. Ask the other children to write the meaning of the new word on their index cards underneath the sentence in which the word appears.

8. Have the children retain these word cards in a word box to which they add on subsequent executions of this activity.

ASSESSMENT   Have the groups teach their words to the other children in the class. Utilize the words the children have compiled into lists for weekly spelling words. In addition to spelling these words, ask the children to write a simple definition for each.

Notes for next time . . .

_____

_____

_____

_____

_____

_____

_____

_____

_____

_____

_____

_____

_____

_____

Cloze Capers

ACTIVITIES TO INCREASE VOCABULARY

SUGGESTED GRADE LEVEL *2–3*

PURPOSE Increase children's ability to comprehend sentences as well as their facility with fine shades of meaning by using this critical-thinking activity.

MATERIALS
- Overhead projector and transparencies
- Brief passages (50–100 words), at children's independent reading level

PROCEDURE

1. Take out either verbs or adjectives from a brief passage, leaving blanks where the words have been deleted. Retain the original passage.

2. Write the following sentence on the overhead transparency: The boys _____ down the street after winning the ball game. Ask the children what action words, or verbs, would best tell how the boys were moving as they went down the street. (Guide the children to see that "cartwheeled" or "leaped" would be more appropriate word choices than "walked" or "strolled.")

3. Read the passage to the children as they follow along, saying "blank" for each of the words that have been deleted.

4. For each blank, invite the children to brainstorm a word that might fit in the blank, soliciting words that best describe the action in the passage, as they did in the example. Decide upon a "best" word for each blank through consensus.

5. When the children have filled in each blank in this manner, read the "new" passage to the children as they follow along. Place the original passage alongside the new passage. Ask the children which passage they prefer and why.

When the children and their father _reached_ the middle of the forest, the father _built_ a good fire. Then the stepmother _demanded,_ "_Wait_ by the fire while we _collect_ fire wood. We will _return_ to collect you later." Hansel _comforted_ Gretel, who became frightened by the dark. Later, they _recalled_ the pebbles that Hansel had _dicsarded._ They _followed_ the pebbles all the way home.

Continued.

6. Divide the class into groups of three. Give them a similar brief passage and, through group discussion, ask them to fill in the missing blanks with appropriate verbs.

7. Have each group read its revised passages and compare the word choices.

Variation:

Try this same activity using deleted adjectives.

ASSESSMENT   After completing the group activity, distribute a third passage with verbs (or adjectives) deleted for the children to complete individually. Assess on the basis of percentage of appropriate words they used.

Notes for next time . . .

_____

_____

_____

_____

_____

_____

_____

_____

_____

_____

Super Word Discoveries

(Adapted from Cunningham, 1998)

10

SUGGESTED GRADE LEVEL *2–3*

PURPOSE For children to stretch the storehouse of words in their reading vocabulary, they can be urged to look for new words, decoding them by using the analogy strategy of comparing them to shorter, known words.

MATERIALS
- A "ballot" for each child, on which to write their discovered word
- A ballot box, in which to collect ballots during the day
- A Word Wall, chart, or bulletin board space on which to retain all the discovered words

PROCEDURE

1. Continue this activity throughout the school year. To introduce the activity, tell the children they are to be looking continually for interesting, unknown words to share with the class. Although they should try to figure out the meaning of the new word by comparing it to words they already know, they may find the meaning by asking someone. Discovered words may come from anywhere—books, newspapers, environmental print, and so on.

2. When children discover a word, they are to write the word on a ballot that is kept in a specific place in the room, put their name under it, and place it in the ballot box.

3. At a certain time at the end of each school day, read all the Super Words aloud to the class.

4. Have the class vote on the word they think is the most interesting, and then ask the child who discovered that word to explain what the word means, how he or she figured it out, and why he or she selected it.

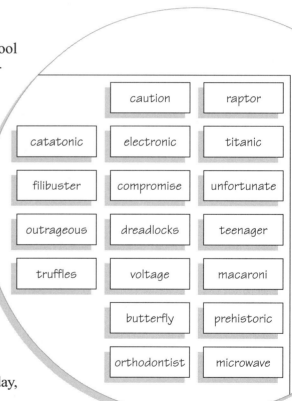

5. Add the Super Word of the day, ceremoniously, to the Word Wall, chart, or bulletin board created for this purpose.

ASSESSMENT Encourage each child to participate in selecting the words, and note how each child attempts to decode unknown words. At various intervals, revisit the Super Word chart and have the children say the words and discuss how other word patterns can help them to decode new words.

Notes for next time . . .

_____

_____

_____

_____

_____

_____

_____

_____

_____

_____

_____

_____

_____

_____

Other Ideas & Activities

- **TORTURE THE TEACHER**
  Have the children take turns daily, finding a new word they think you will not know. Have them write their word on the top righthand corner of the chalkboard while you decide whether you know it or not. (Tell them the definition, simply, if you know it.) Keep a running tally of the words you know and the words you miss, showing the children that even teachers can learn new words!

- **DESCRIBE THE OBJECT**
  Place a common object (e.g., scissors) in a bag and give it to a volunteer, who peeks in the bag. Have that child use words to describe the object without naming it. From the child's description, other children may try to draw the object or simply guess what it is.

- **FAVORITE WORDS**
  Share your favorite word(s) with the children and encourage them to collect their own favorites. Keep a tally of these words on a prominently displayed Word Wall.

- **WORD BANKS**
  On colored 3" × 5" cards, have the children write new words they encounter in reading or in discussions. Provide time in class to discuss these words.

- **HINKY PINKY**
  Provide clues for words that are rhyming synonyms, such as "a small insect" (wee bee) or "an unhappy father" (sad dad). When the children are facile at figuring them out, have them create their own.

- **PICTURE DICTIONARIES**
  Have the children create and alphabetize their own colorful picture dictionaries for new words they have learned. This is especially helpful for ELL children.

- **WORDS FROM OTHER LANGUAGES**
  As words are encountered through reading and discussion, collect them from other languages and cultures (e.g., bazaar, ballet, fiesta, patio). Have the children make a bulletin board illustrating these words and their country of origin.

- **BEANBAG PREFIXES**
  Select a common prefix (e.g., in, re, sub, un, com) and ask the children to think of a word that begins with this word part as you throw a beanbag to them. Allow them to get help from a classmate. When ideas have been exhausted, change the prefix. Write new words on a Word Wall.

- **WHAT'S THIS WORD?**
Daily, ask the children to bring in words they have heard or seen for which they would like to know the meaning. Utilize these words in your weekly spelling list.

- **PASSWORD**
Select one student to be "it" and have that child face the class, away from the board. Select a vocabulary word that has been recently introduced and write it on the board. Have other children try to help the chosen child guess the word by providing synonyms for the word. Write these synonyms on the board and discuss them after someone has guessed the word.

- **WORD OF THE DAY**
Choose a "stretch" word that is just above the children's meaning vocabulary. Explain its meaning and offer a small prize to every child who uses that word correctly during the day, either orally or in written form. Example: procrastination.

- **WORD PICTURE HUNT**
Challenge the children to find pictures from old magazines that illustrate their new vocabulary—e.g., a picture of a desert might illustrate the word "desolate"; a picture of a cat watching goldfish might illustrate the word "captivating." Make "pictionary" scrapbooks from these pictures.

- **LISTENING WALKS**
Take children on a listening walk around the school. Tell them to be very quiet as they listen to the rhythms of the cafeteria, office, playground, and so forth. When they return to the classroom, have them use a variety of juicy words to describe the sounds they heard.

- **CATEGORIES**
Invite one child to choose a category, such as trees, or cars. Other children take turns contributing a word that fits the category. When children have finished offering as many words as they can think of, the words are written down and categorized.

Children's Literature List

Antoine, Heloise, illustrated by Ingrid Godon. *Curious Kids Go on Vacation: Another Big Book of Words* (Atlanta: Peachtree, 1997).

A delightful book written in the format of a themed pictionary, exploring a family vacation. More than 40 small objects are labeled, each relating to something one does or needs on a vacation.

Gwynne, Fred. *Chocolate Moose for Dinner.* (New York: Simon & Schuster, 1976).

A hilarious book featuring a compendium of familiar expressions that are often confusing to young children, such as "We need to set up a *car pool*," and "Lions *prey* on other animals." Colorful illustrations show what children hear from the expressions. The book can lead to discussion about the expressions, and the children can create another book with other expressions that confuse them.

Kessler, Leonard. *Old Turtle's Riddle and Joke Book.* (New York: Greenwillow, 1986).

Favorite riddles, which include classics such as: What fish chase mice? Cat fish. What happens when ducks fly? They quack up. Reinforces awareness of multiple meanings of words.

Most, Bernard. *Pets in Trumpets and Other Word-Play Riddles.* (New York: Harcourt, 1991).

Riddles with the answer to each as the key word in the riddle and bold-faced in the text: Why did the musician find a dog in his trumpet? Because he always finds a **pet** in his trumpet. Reinforces seeking pronounceable word chunks in words.

Young, Selina. *My Favorite Word Book: Words and Pictures for the Very Young.* (New York: Random House, 1999).

An irresistible introduction to words and reading by Zoe and Toby. More than 500 nouns are depicted in detailed drawings that feature an adorable cast of recurring characters. Can be used to build vocabulary, especially for ELL, in an enjoyable way.

Other Resources for Teaching Vocabulary

Classrooms That Work: They Can All Read and Write, by Patricia M. Cunningham (New York: Addison-Wesley, 1998).

Loaded with classroom strategies and activities to teach children to read and write through extensive exploration of the English language in an enjoyable way.

Easy Mini-Lessons for Building Vocabulary: Practical Strategies That Boost Word Knowledge and Reading Comprehension, by Laura Robb (Jefferson City, VA: Scholastic Professional Books, 1998).

Mini-lessons and activities covering vocabulary discussion charts, linking new words to children's lives, learning about roots, prefixes, and suffixes, conquering contextual clues, building word banks, and other strategies.

Let the Shadows Speak: Developing Children's Language Through Shadow Puppetry, by Franzeska Ewart (Herndon, VA: Stylus Publishing, 1998).

Intended for teachers who are looking for exciting and effective ways to help children express themselves and enhance their vocabulary, be they bilingual children, children with language difficulties, or gifted children bored with traditional approaches.

Literature-Based Reading Activities, by Hallie Kay and Ruth Helen Yopp (Boston: Allyn & Bacon, 1996).

Uses children's literature as a vehicle through which to reinforce vocabulary development as well as personal response to what is read.

Teaching Vocabulary in All Classrooms, by Camille Blachowicz and Peter Fisher (Englewood Cliffs, NJ: Merrill, 1996).

Explores independent means of learning vocabulary and the value of word play, as well as teacher-directed techniques that have the broader goal of enhancing the acquisition of new knowledge.

What's In a Word? Vocabulary Development in Multilingual Classrooms, by Norah McWilliams (Herndon, VA: Stylus Publishing, 1998).

Develops children's word power. This book offers practical approaches and strategies based on the linguistic, cognitive, and social principles affecting children's use of words and their meanings in English as an acquired language.

Word Matters: Teaching Phonics and Spelling in the Reading/Writing Classroom, by Gay Su Pinnell, Irene Fountas, and Mary Ellen Giacobbe (New York: Heinemann, 1998).

Word study leading to enhancement of reading vocabulary; offers many strategies to help children learn to decode and remember words.

In Closing

1. After using the activities in this section, what insights have you gained about how children acquire vocabulary? What did you discover about yourself as a teacher of literacy by teaching these activities?

2. Which of the activities in the section did you think were particularly effective for the following types of vocabulary development? Why?

   - Learning new words for new concepts

   - Enriching the meaning of known words

   - Learning new words for known concepts

   - Moving words into children's speaking vocabulary

   - Learning new meanings for known words

3. Which activities did you think best encouraged the love of language? In what ways was this manifested?

4. Which activity did you think was most successful in developing children's ability to use the context to figure out the meaning of unknown words? Why?

5. Select an activity that offered you the most insights into the level of vocabulary development of your learners. What did you discover? Cite examples of specific children with whom you worked.

6. Several of the activities used a combination of senses to help children remember words that were introduced. What might be the advantages and disadvantages of these activities? What did you learn about the learning styles of specific children through these activities?

7. Several of the activities focused on having children use more colorful words and phrases either orally or in writing. How will such vocabulary enrichment activities help children to become better writers? Why do you think so?

8. Certain activities asked children to consider the fine shades of meaning of words they already knew. How is speaking and writing vocabulary enhanced as a result of these activities? Why do you think so?

9. Which activities were most difficult for your ELL children? What did you observe about their difficulties? How could you revise these activities to make them more accessible to your ELL children?

10. Identify a child you think has a highly developed meaning vocabulary. What are the characteristics of that child? Did his or her behavior during the activities differ from that of other children? Describe the differences, if any.

6

ACTIVITIES TO FOSTER READING COMPREHENSION

Introduction

Since before the turn of the 20th century, educators have been touting reading comprehension as an integral part of reading and have attempted to understand exactly what happens when a reader comprehends. With exciting new research into how the brain functions during reading, the interest in this phenomenon is perhaps greater than ever. But the process of comprehension itself has not changed—we simply have a more sophisticated understanding of comprehension and an even greater need for literate, critical thinkers who are prepared to participate in an increasingly complex world.

Once thought of as simply the natural result of decoding plus oral language, comprehension now is viewed as a much more complicated process resulting from an interface among background knowledge, experience, critical thinking, and direct instruction. Comprehension currently is defined as *the construction of meaning from text* and is the ultimate goal of exemplary, balanced literacy instruction. Proficient readers and beginning readers, too, construct meaning by making connections—by integrating what they know about a topic with what they are immediately encountering in print.

Proficient readers possess a myriad of strategies from which they can select to help them interact with text and construct meaning. These strategies must be directly taught to beginning readers through modeling, guided practice, and plenty of independent application with reading material. In addition, young children must receive the opportunity to share their personal responses to what they read, in a variety of social settings.

The activities in this section have been chosen to foster comprehension in children who are in the early stages of literacy development. Some activities are appropriate for children with limited decoding skills, by promoting listening comprehension through read-alouds. Other activities require some decoding skill and are appropriate only for children who can read independently.

Opinionaires

(Adapted from Readence, Bean, & Baldwin, 1998)

SUGGESTED GRADE LEVEL *2–3*

PURPOSE

This prereading structured activity provides children with a statement with which children must agree or disagree. By focusing on this statement, which is related to key ideas or issues in the passage to be read, the teacher can provide connections with children's prior knowledge on the subject to be introduced and show the children graphically how reading and the new information it provides can change minds.

MATERIALS

- Overhead transparency or chart paper (showing a somewhat controversial statement)
- Two pieces of paper for each child

PROCEDURE

1. From a text that is about to be read to or by the children, create a provocative idea or piece of misinformation.

2. Write a statement concerning this topic on the overhead transparency or chart paper and read it to the children. For example, if the passage offers children information about garden snakes, the statement might be "All snakes are bad."

   All snakes are bad.

   ◯ I agree   ⊗ I disagree

3. Divide the children into small share groups of three to four children each and ask them to discuss the statement.

4. Give each child a piece of paper and ask the children to decide whether they agree or disagree with the statement. More proficient writers may be asked to write down their individual opinion regarding the statement. Preliterate children might draw a happy face indicating that they agree or a sad face indicating disagreement with the statement.

5. Explain to the children that they will be reading (or listening to) a passage that contains information about the topic that has just been discussed. Ask them to read (or listen) to the passage to see what the author has to say about the topic.

6. Afterward, hand out to each child a paper upon which is written the same statement. Have the children reconsider the statement and write down their answer.

7. Conduct a whole-group discussion asking children if their feelings about the topic have changed after their reading. Encourage them to explain exactly what caused them to change their minds.

ASSESSMENT   Note whether the opinion of each child changed. Ask each to orally defend his or her position to you, changed or unchanged, on the basis of what he or she read (heard).

Notes for next time . . .

_____

_____

_____

_____

_____

_____

_____

_____

_____

_____

_____

_____

_____

Sentence Pantomimes

SUGGESTED GRADE LEVEL *2–3*

PURPOSE   Research and observation have determined that certain language structures, especially those with indirect objects or adverbial clauses, may cause comprehension difficulties, especially for children for whom English is a second language. Reflecting on their knowledge of language and focusing on these structures, as this language activity does, can improve children's comprehension of difficult sentences.

MATERIALS   ● 10 sentence cards containing sentences with clauses and indirect objects (see illustration).

PROCEDURE

1. Divide children into groups of three.

2. Read all of the sentences to the children without explaining their meaning, just to be sure the children can properly decode all the words.

3. Distribute one sentence card to each group and ask the groups to discuss how they might act out their sentence for the rest of the class. Have each group select one group member to read the sentence while the other two act it out.

4. Call on the groups, one at a time, to come up to the front of the room and act out their sentence card for the rest of the class as one member of their group reads it.

5. Ask the rest of the class to show, by a "thumbs up" or a "thumbs down" signal, whether they think the actors correctly interpreted the meaning of the sentence.

As Fred looked out the window, Nan scratched her head.

Bob put on his hat after Candy rang the bell.

Ann told Jim to give the pencil to the teacher.

Bill sat down before Cara started to sing.

While Jon was whistling a tune, Cindy was smiling.

Before Brian turned around, Tina was in his seat.

Mark told Mary to give the pen to Sue.

Because Lisa gave me a book, I told her, "Thank you!"

Until Ryan stands up, Linda will not clap her hands.

Rita will hum a tune as Jose waves to the rest of the class.

6. If any children disagree with the interpretation, invite them individually to reenact the sentence as they think it should be. Discuss their interpretation.

ASSESSMENT   Because this exercise does not require reading or speaking, it can be used as an informal evaluation of receptive language for children in their "silent period" of language development. Ask individual children to act out each sentence as you say it. Particularly note problems that ELL children encounter.

Notes for next time . . .

_____

_____

_____

_____

_____

_____

_____

_____

_____

_____

_____

_____

_____

_____

Which One Am I?

**SUGGESTED
GRADE LEVEL** *2–3*

PURPOSE
Proficient readers verify their predictions as they read. Knowing that their predictions were on target provides positive reinforcement. This activity allows children to preview a story and make predictions about what the characters are like and encourages them to check their predictions after reading.

MATERIALS
- Three large poster boards, each containing a description of a character in a story
- Black marker
- Writing paper for each child in the class

PROCEDURE

1. Prior to the reading of the selection, write on one of the poster boards a detailed description of the internal qualities of the main character in a story children are about to read. On each of the other two boards, write a detailed description that does not describe this character.

2. Choose a child to read each of the three descriptions.

3. Have the three children come to the front of the classroom and take turns reading their descriptions aloud, then holding them up for all to see.

4. Ask the class to decide which of the three descriptions they think might describe the main character in the story they are about to read.

5. Ask the children to each write a sentence telling why they chose the description they did.

6. Ask the children to read [listen to] the story to find clues that validate or invalidate their original descriptions as they learn about the main character.

Continued.

7. Following the reading, have the same three children return to the front of the class and reread the descriptions so the children can revise their opinions.

8. Lead a discussion about which clues in the story caused the children to change their mind or validate their original opinion. Have them find evidence in the story to support their revised opinions.

ASSESSMENT Ask the children to write a sentence or two stating how they know the description of the main character is now correct. Encourage them to copy evidence directly from the story.

Notes for next time . . .

_____

_____

_____

_____

_____

_____

_____

_____

_____

_____

_____

_____

_____

Which Came First?

SUGGESTED
GRADE LEVEL   *2–3*

PURPOSE   Causal relationships are some of the most difficult to discern for early readers, especially for Second Language Learners. The following activity will help to promote an awareness of cause and effect relationships in sentences through small group problem solving and discussion.

MATERIALS
- Chalkboard and chalk
- 10 sentence strips (see illustration)

PROCEDURE

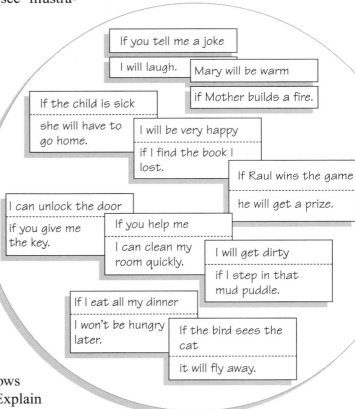

1. Write the following sentence on the chalkboard: If it rains, we will not play ball. Discuss which event comes first, the rain or the decision not to play ball.

2. Explain that the word "if" often signals something that "causes" something else to happen, and that event is called the "effect."

3. Provide another example: I will give you a penny if you say "please."

4. Ask the children to tell you what follows the word "if." (You say "please.") Explain that this is the cause. Ask the children to tell you what the effect will be. (I will give you a penny.)

5. Read the 10 sentence strips to children. While they watch, cut each sentence strip apart between the cause and the effect.

Continued.

6. Divide the children into groups of three. Distribute two unmatched sentence halves to each group.

7. After they have read the nonsensical sentence they were given, ask the children to visit other groups, trying to locate the matching half of their sentence.

8. When all have found their matched sentences, ask them to read their sentence to the rest of the class, explaining which part is the cause and which is the effect.

ASSESSMENT   Individually, ask the children to complete each sentence when you give them the first part, using the 10 sentences in the illustration. The endings need not be exact as long as they make sense. Then ask the children to tell you which part of each sentence is the "cause" and which is the "effect." Tally the number of correct responses.

Notes for next time . . .

_____

_____

_____

_____

_____

_____

_____

_____

_____

Story Imaging

SUGGESTED GRADE LEVEL *1–3*

PURPOSE   Proficient readers "see" the characters, setting, and events contained in print by imaging. This activity gives children practice in re-creating a story using their "mind's eye," practicing crucial sequencing skills at the same time.

MATERIALS   ● A story board (paper divided into six panels) for each child

PROCEDURE

1. Gather the children on the floor around you. Instruct the children to close their eyes and make their mind as empty as possible.

2. Ask them to try to recall the first event of a story they recently have read (heard). Ask them to raise their hand as soon as they can "see" the event in their mind.

3. When all hands are up, solicit responses as to what individual children have visualized, and encourage them to elaborate on their images.

4. Repeat these steps with the rest of the events in the story.

5. Working individually or in small share groups, ask the children to draw the events they have visualized, using the spaces in the story board, in order of their occurrence.

6. Have the children take turns retelling the story, using the pictures on their story boards as prompts.

Variation:

Instead of having the children draw the events in the story, have them retell the story speaking into a tape recorder.

ASSESSMENT   Make a checklist containing all the features of narrative structure as they have been taught to the children—beginning, middle, end; characters, setting, plot, events, ending, and so on. As individual children share their story boards, assess their ability to retell the story, using the checklist as a guide.

Notes for next time . . .

_____

_____

_____

_____

_____

_____

_____

Mindscape

SUGGESTED
GRADE LEVEL *2–3*

PURPOSE Comprehension deepens when children are able to elaborate on a text by adding information to their preexisting knowledge. This activity allows children to elaborate on a story by inferring what selected characters were thinking as they were presented in various capacities.

MATERIALS
- An outline of a head, with lines for writing inside, one for each child
- Crayons or colored markers

PROCEDURE

1. After reading a narrative text with the children, ask them to discuss their favorite parts of the story.

2. Pass out a head outline to each child. Ask the children to choose a favorite character from the story. Explain that they will decorate the outline to match the outside of this character's head.

3. Pass out crayons or colored markers and encourage the children to make the outline look like their chosen character by adding the appropriate colored and styled hair, a hat, bow, or other features that symbolize the person.

4. Ask the children to revisit the story to find a favorite part that contains their character. Instruct them to copy a sentence from this part, placing it underneath the character's head.

5. Ask the children: What was [your character] thinking while this was going on? Imagine what he/she was saying to himself/herself and write your ideas on the lines inside his/her head.

Those silly children are not going to steal my broom. I'll do something mean to them.

"I'm going to make you wish you were a black cat."

6 *Mindscape*

Continued.

6. Have the children share their Mindscape with the rest of the class, reading the excerpt and telling how they think the character was feeling at that time and why they think so.

ASSESSMENT Check for each child's ability to: (1) find an excerpt that relates to his or her chosen character, and (2) appropriately infer how that character might be feeling in the situation.

Notes for next time . . .

_____

_____

_____

_____

_____

_____

_____

_____

_____

_____

_____

_____

_____

_____

_____

Handy Reading

SUGGESTED GRADE LEVEL *2–3*

PURPOSE
This activity addresses two issues common to early readers: (1) the tendency to read all the text at the same rate, and (2) the lack of monitoring their own understanding. The reader must retell what has been read, increasing metacognitive awareness. The activity is especially useful with expository texts.

MATERIALS
- Copies of identical text for each pair of children

PROCEDURE

1. Divide the children into partners and have them sit side by side. Explain that in the activity they are about to do, they will be asked to retell everything they read.

2. Ask them to place their right hand over the beginning of the text. Tell them that the amount that was covered is the part they will read first.

3. Instruct them to silently read the small amount of text and then actually cover it with their right hand.

4. Ask the children to look up and try to remember, in their head, what they just read.

5. Instruct the children to turn to their partner and take turns telling what they remember from their reading, adding to each other's remembrances to create a more complete picture of the text.

6. Have the children read another "handful" of text silently and repeat the retelling step.

7. Instruct them to continue in this fashion until the text has been read and retold entirely.

Continued.

ASSESSMENT   Using the above procedure, ask the children, one by one, to read to you from a similar text and retell sections of it after the same short intervals. Note their ability to reconstruct key ideas and supporting details.

Notes for next time . . .

_____

_____

_____

_____

_____

_____

_____

_____

_____

_____

_____

_____

_____

_____

_____

_____

Flip Book Summaries

(Adapted from Linda Hoyt, Revisit, Reflect, Retell, 1999)

ACTIVITIES TO FOSTER READING COMPREHENSION

SUGGESTED GRADE LEVEL   1—3

PURPOSE   The ability to retell, or summarize, is an important component of reading comprehension. This activity asks children to retell a story in written form in the sequence in which the events happened.

MATERIALS
- 9" × 12" white construction paper, precut (see illustration)
- Markers or colored pencils

PROCEDURE

1. After reading a narrative text to the children, make four columns on the chalkboard, labeled *title, beginning, middle,* and *end.*

2. Have the children brainstorm events that occurred in each of these parts of the story.

3. Model a finished example of the flip book; explain that the title and author will go in the first box, something that happened in the beginning will go in the second box, something that happened in the middle will go in the third box, something that happened at the end of the story will be put in the final box.

4. When they flip the flap on each box, have them draw a picture that goes with the words they chose.

5. Have the children share their words and drawings with the rest of the class, telling why they chose the parts to tell about and draw.

ASSESSMENT   Evaluate the finished flip book for each child on the basis of sequential order and the presence of a title page, beginning part, middle part, and ending part. With preliterate children, oral presentations regarding the illustrations can be used to determine if the children understand the basics of story structure.

The boy sees a dog in the clouds. He is at the beach.	The dog becomes real and the boy and dog play. The mom says to try to find the owner.	The boy gets to keep the dog.

THE SKY DOG

by

Brinton Turkle

Notes for next time . . .

_____

_____

_____

_____

_____

_____

_____

Consequences

ACTIVITIES TO FOSTER READING COMPREHENSION

SUGGESTED GRADE LEVEL   *2–3*

PURPOSE   This activity helps children to reflect on the behavior shown by a main character in stories they have read, to identify with that character's reasons for behaving a certain way, and finally, to consider the consequences of that behavior.

MATERIALS
- Chalkboard or overhead transparency

PROCEDURE

1. Place four boxes horizontally on the chalkboard or overhead transparency. Over the first box, write the word "Character." Over the second, write "Behavior." Over the third box, write "Why?". Over the fourth box, write "Result."

2. Invite the children to consider the behavior of a main character in a favorite story the children have read, using this graphic organizer. For example, have children recall Goldilocks and put her name in the first box. What words might be used to tell about the behavior of Goldilocks in the story of Goldilocks and the Three Bears? (Naughty; disobedient; she went where she wasn't supposed to.) Write these words in the second box. For the third box, ask the children to consider why Goldilocks behaved the way she did. For example, they may believe she was just bored, or that she was looking for an adventure. Accept all reasonable responses. To fill in the fourth box, ask the children to think about the result of boxes two and three. For example, if the children said Goldilocks was naughty because she was bored, what was the result of this naughty behavior? (She trespassed in the bears' house and got chased.) Write the answer in the fourth box.

Character	Behavior
Gingerbread Boy	runs away

Why?	Result
wants to run and play	gets eaten

3. Erase the boxes and begin the process again using a character from a different story. Have the children work in groups of three to consider their answers for each of the boxes. Then call on groups to contribute their responses.

ASSESSMENT Make a checklist for each child. Include the categories "character," "behavior," "reason," and "result." Using a similar story that all children have read, assess each child's ability to determine a reasonable response for each category.

Notes for next time . . .

_____

_____

_____

_____

_____

_____

_____

_____

_____

_____

_____

_____

_____

_____

_____

Sentence Sharing

(Adapted from Tompkins, 50 Literacy Strategies, 1998)   ACTIVITIES TO FOSTER READING COMPREHENSION

**SUGGESTED
GRADE LEVEL**   *2–3*

PURPOSE   In this social activity, the teacher selects the excerpts for the children to read in order to introduce or review important concepts, summarize events, or focus on an element of expository structure. The activity also provides an authentic purpose for repeated reading to develop fluency.

MATERIALS   • Oaktag sentence strips containing key ideas from text

PROCEDURE

1. Ahead of time, make sentence strips on oaktag from an informational book or content-area textbook that the children have read. Include only key ideas from the text and make each sentence meaningful by itself (see examples on the next page).

2. Distribute sentence strips to individual children, or have them work in pairs. Ask them to practice reading (help them with difficult words) their strip until they can read it fluently and confidently.

3. Instruct the students to move around the classroom, stopping to read their excerpt to another child in the class. When they have chosen a reading buddy, they sit elbow to elbow, taking turns reading their excerpts to each other.

4. After the first child reads, the two children discuss the text that has been read. Then the other child reads and the two discuss the second excerpt.

5. When the partners have finished reading, they disband, search for other partners, and repeat the procedure.

6. When most children have finished, have them return to their seats. Invite volunteers to read their excerpts to the rest of the class and share what they have learned through the Sentence Share activity.

ASSESSMENT   Take anecdotal notes on the progress individual children have made between the first and final reading of their text excerpt. In addition, you might ask them to recall as much as they can about the text from participating in the activity.

Sentence Strips

Trees are the tallest and oldest living things on earth.

Many redwood trees are more than 2,500 years old.

A young tree may have a trunk no bigger around than your thumb.

The tallest trees in the United States are the giant sequoias and redwoods in California.

The trunk is attached to a big tangle of roots that are crooked and reach out in every direction.

Some sequoias have such big trunks that it would take twenty men to make a circle around them!

One of the most valuable uses of trees is in making houses and furniture out of the wood.

The number of rings extending outward from the center of its trunk tell how old a tree is.

The trunk of a tree grows longer and bigger around as the tree gets taller and heavier.

The tree is made up of three parts—the trunk, the roots, and the branches.

Most of a tree's roots are buried below the surface of the ground.

Roots are made of wood like the trunk and the overhead branches.

Sometimes you can see the top of a tree's root above ground.

Notes for next time . . .

_____

_____

_____

_____

_____

_____

Other Ideas & Activities

- **MIX-UP**
  Print the main ideas of a story on oaktag strips and place the strips in incorrect order in a pocket chart. Ask the children to read each strip aloud while putting the strips in the correct order according to the sequence of events in the story.

- **TRUE OR FALSE?**
  Prepare several statements about a story that has just been read, some true and some false. Give each child two cards—one labeled *true* and the other labeled *false*. As you read each statement aloud, ask the children to hold up the appropriate card.

- **RATE IT**
  Encourage the children to think critically about the books they have read. With your guidance, invite the children to establish their own rating system for books they have read—from poor (a sad face) to excellent (a happy face).

- **PROBLEM SOLVING**
  In small groups, have the children respond to the following questions concerning problems of the main characters in stories they have recently read: What problem did the main character face? How did he/she solve the problem? How would you have solved the problem?

- **FAVORITE SCENES**
  Have the children depict scenes from books they have read, using papier mache, fabric, construction paper, clay, or other materials. Encourage each child to share his or her creation with the class, describing the events that led up to the scene as well as those that followed it.

- **INFERENCES**
  Bring in an old gardening or driving glove. Ask the children to make inferences about who might have owned it by examining it (e.g., if it is for the right hand, a right-handed person may have taken it off to pull a weed and lost it; if it is large, it may belong to an adult man, etc.).

- **PICTURE DIARY**
  Have the children make a picture diary for their favorite character in a story that has been read recently, by drawing four things that happened in the story in order, folded into four parts on construction paper.

- **CONTRAST CHART**
  Give each child a paper containing two columns, one labeled *likenesses* and the other *differences*. Have the children compare two stories that were read recently, considering factors such as setting, number of characters, mood, difficulty, and others.

- **MAIN IDEA DRAWINGS**

  Ask the children to use just one drawing to best tell what a story they have just read or heard is about. Invite them to share their drawing with the class, telling how their drawing captures the main idea of the story.

- **SHADOW PUPPETS**

  With tagboard and black markers, have the children trace the main characters from a book they have read, cut them out, and tape straightened-out paper clips to the back. Using the overhead projector, have them retell the story with the help of these shadow puppets.

- **TAPED BOOK CHAT**

  Ask the children to tape-record their reactions to a book they have read. Encourage them to tell just enough to interest their classmates and make them curious but not so much that they don't need to read the book for themselves.

- **PREDICT THE ENDING**

  Read a provocative book aloud to the children. Stop at the most exciting part. Ask the children to brainstorm what they think will happen next. Have them listen to confirm or refute their hunches.

- **STORY-PICTURE SEQUENCING**

  Prepare a sequence of pictures that tell a story from discarded basals or trade books. Read the story to children and then have them arrange the pictures and retell the story in the correct sequence.

- **INTERVIEWS**

  Have children pretend to be reporters and interview a favorite movie star, sports star, recording star, and so forth. Ask them to create a list of five questions they might ask and then predict the answers the person might give.

Children's Literature List

Appelt, Kathi, illustrated by Keith Baker. *Elephants Aloft.* (New York: Harcourt Brace, 1993).

An adventurous journey of two elephants named Rama and Raja from India to Africa to visit their aunt. One adjective on every two-page spread describes what is happening. An excellent book for a read/listen and retell.

Bridwell, Norman. *Clifford and the Big Parade.* (New York: Cartwheel/Scholastic, 1998).

Popular Clifford again saving the day in his own unique way. Children will enjoy guessing what will happen as Clifford and Emily participate in their town's birthday celebration. An ideal book for having children predict the outcome.

Dumphy, Madeleine, illustrated by Alan James Robinson. *Here Is the Arctic Winter.* (New York: Hyperion, 1993).

A beautifully illustrated expository text explaining how some animals are strong enough to survive the cold, dark Arctic winter while others are not. An excellent model for young readers for an introduction to expository text using comparison and contrast.

Flournoy, Valerie. *Tanya's Reunion.* (New York: Dial, 1995).

The travels of Tanya and her grandmother to an old farm in Virginia to attend a family reunion is a pencil-and-watercolor-illustrated picture story book. Because the story's dialogue is so rich in rural African American dialect, the story is great for creating a Reader's Theatre with children.

Wildsmith, Brian, and Wildsmith, Rebecca. *Wake Up, Wake Up.* (New York: Harcourt, 1993).

Practice with cause and effect relationships. Rooster starts a chain reaction by waking one animal which wakes up another animal, and so on until the last animal wakes up the farmer, who feeds them all.

Other Resources for Fostering Comprehension

Asking Better Questions: Models, Techniques, and Activities for Engaging Students in Learning, by Norah Morgan and Juliana Saxton (York, ME: Stenhouse Publishers, 1996).

Simple examples showing K–8 teachers how they can pose well thought-out questions to children and in turn encourage children to ask themselves better questions. Teachers learn to use questions to acquire information about students, build common knowledge, and increase comprehension.

Better Books! Better Readers! How to Choose, Use, and Level Books for Children in the Primary Grades, by Linda Hart-Hewins and Jan Wells (York, ME: Stenhouse Publishers, 1999).

Based on the authors' belief that using real books and real writing experiences help children not only become literate but also lovers of reading. Offers practical guidelines for creating classrooms that foster language learning and critical thinking.

Content Area Literacy: An Integrated Approach, by John E. Readence, Thomas W. Bean, and R. Scott Baldwin (Dubuque, IA: Kendall/Hunt, 1998).

Explores the development of reading comprehension strategies throughout the curriculum. Though most are suitable for older students, some are appropriate for grades 2–3.

50 Literacy Strategies: Step by Step, by Gail E. Tompkins (New York: Merrill, 1998).

Some of the best known and most effective strategies for teaching reading and writing K–6 in an easy-to-follow format. Spiral bound.

Keeping It Together: Linking Reading Theory to Practice, by Ian Morrison (Bothell, WA: Wright Group, 1996).

Especially for early elementary students, links proven classroom practices with a consistent theory of reading and comprehension in a practical way.

Reading Strategies that Work: Teaching Your Students to Become Better Readers, by Laura Robb (Jefferson City, MO: Scholastic Professional Books, 1998).

A set of more than 30 strategies that proficient readers use. Included are strategies for predicting, summarizing, rereading, inferring, and noting cause and effect.

Revisit, Reflect, and Retell: Strategies for Improving Reading Comprehension, by Linda Hoyt (Westport, CT: Heinemann, 1999).

A highly practical collection of more than 130 strategies and 90 reproducibles for any teacher attempting to evoke high-quality response to literature. It explores why readers should respond to text, when they should respond, and how they might be invited to respond in authentic ways.

Tell Me: Children, Reading, and Talk, by Aidan Chambers (York, ME: Stenhouse Publishers, 1996).

An approach for discussing books so children learn to find the heart of a story, make sense of a string of facts, and understand important ideas. Practical information about booktalking, explaining some of the processes and outlining the ground rules developed by teachers and others who work with children and books.

In Closing

1. After using the activities in this section, what insights have you gained about how children develop reading and listening comprehension skills? What did you discover about yourself as a teacher of literacy by teaching these activities?

2. Which of the activities in this section did you find were particularly effective in teaching the following comprehension strategies? Why?

   - Making predictions

   - Visualizing

   - Tuning in to prior knowledge

   - Making personal connections

   - Monitoring understanding

   - Generalizing

   - Evaluating

   - Asking and answering questions

3. Choose an activity that was particularly easy and one that was difficult for the children with whom you worked. Why do you think it was easy/difficult? What, if any, adaptations would you make next time you teach the lesson? Why?

4. What did you discover about the need to determine what children already know about a subject before beginning an instructional activity? How did the assessment suggestions at the end of each activity provide you with insights into the strengths and limitations of your teaching of comprehension strategies?

5. Select an activity that offered you the most insights into the general knowledge background of the children with whom you worked. What did you discover about the importance of children having background knowledge about a topic before reading? Cite examples of specific children with whom you worked.

6. Several of the activities asked children to retell narratives after reading. What comprehension strategies are reinforced and assessed through the use of these activities? What did you learn about your learners' comprehension as a result of doing these activities?

7. Certain activities encouraged children to figure out deleted words by using the context of the sentence. What might be the advantages and disadvantages of these activities? What did you learn about a specific child's use of comprehension strategies based upon these activities?

8. Some activities asked children to revisit a favorite character after reading and write something about that character. How do you think reading comprehension can be developed through the use of these activities? Why? Give examples of specific children and what you think they learned as a result of this activity.

9. Which activities seemed especially difficult for your ELL children? What did you observe about their difficulties? How could you revise these activities to make them more accessible to your ELL children?

10. Identify a child you think has a highly developed ability to use comprehension strategies. What are the characteristics of that child? Did his or her behavior during the activities differ from that of other children? Describe the differences, if any.

7

ACTIVITIES TO INSPIRE YOUNG WRITERS

Introduction

Reading and writing provide the major paths to literacy for young children. Children learn the value of communication through the written word early on—long before they enter school—as they struggle to make sense of print in their environment. From posters on nursery room walls, to before-bedtime story books, to billboards inundating the community, letters and words soon become part of the consciousness of young children. Their need to know what the words say compels them first out of curiosity, quickly replaced by the desire to communicate themselves. The acquisition of reading and writing then enables children to develop into individuals capable of communicating in unique and personal ways.

Early attempts at writing provide opportunities for children to experiment with print and extend their understanding of text. It follows that emergent writing—if much experimentation is encouraged—has been found to play a pivotal role in children's learning to read. Experimentation provides children with invaluable practice with segmenting sounds into words, leading to an understanding of the relationship between sounds and letters, or phonics.

Writing activities go beyond the skills and mechanics and can be the catalyst for the natural interaction of language acquisition and development. Moreover, writing activities following reading can enhance and improve reading comprehension, as composition is an interactive process that challenges the writer to construct meaning for an intended audience. The author/reader relationship contained in writing is essential to reading comprehension because the author is responsible for making the writing comprehensible to others.

Rather than developing *after* learning how to read, as educators once assumed, we now know that writing can accompany and enhance the young child's growing interest in naming letters and reading print. The following activities have been selected to accommodate young children's wishes to quickly read and write by providing them with authentic opportunities to participate in motivational writing purposes.

Text Template

(Adapted from Readence, Bean, & Baldwin, 1998)

SUGGESTED GRADE LEVEL   *1–3*

PURPOSE   With the right provocative questions, children can tap into their imagination to create interesting text. The following activity is guaranteed to get very young children engaged in brainstorming and writing original text.

MATERIALS
- A large box wrapped in brown paper
- Text templates (see illustration)
- Crayons or colored pencils

PROCEDURE

1. Wrap a large box in brown paper and write in large letters on the sides: Danger! Do not open! Caution! Be very careful!

2. Allow the box to sit in the classroom for a day while the children wonder what is in it and generate questions about its possible contents. Explain that you will talk about the box at a later time.

3. On a later date, gather the children for a group brainstorming session about what might be in the box. As children have had time to allow their imagination to run wild, they probably will have many ideas in response to the following questions:

    Where do you think the box came from?

    What might happen if we open it?

    What do you think is in the box?

    Why is the box here?

4. Pass out the text templates. Explain to the children that they are to put their ideas on the paper in response to each of the questions.

THE MYSTERY BOX

I think the box came from
_____.

If we open the box, _____.
_____.

I think _____ is in the box.

The box is here because _____
_____.

5. Read the text templates with the children. Ask them to complete the sentences with their own ideas (more advanced writers may be encouraged to deviate from the template format or write an entire story of their own creation). Encourage them to use invented, or temporary, spelling for unfamiliar words.

6. When the children have finished writing, invite them to draw a picture of the contents they believe to be in the box.

ASSESSMENT   Evaluate the children's writing on the basis of appropriateness of answers to the questions. Also note each child's ability to map sounds using the appropriate letters and letter combinations, based on the child's spelling stage.

Notes for next time . . .

_____

_____

_____

_____

_____

_____

_____

_____

_____

_____

_____

_____

Quick Write

2

SUGGESTED GRADE LEVEL   *2–3*

PURPOSE   Writing that takes place before reading can help young children clarify what they have learned and helps them respond later to what they have read. Writing before reading also encourages children to think about what they are reading.

MATERIALS
- Timer
- Writing utensils
- Writing paper

PROCEDURE

1. Before introducing the children to an expository piece on a topic such as cows, tell them that you are going to give them 2 minutes to write down everything they know about cows (preliterate children may draw pictures illustrating their knowledge).

2. Tell the children to list as many ideas as they can think of and not to worry about spelling, handwriting, or creating complete sentences.

3. Set the timer for 2 minutes and tell the children to begin writing.

4. When the time is up, ask the children to draw a line after their last idea and then count the total number of ideas they wrote down about the topic.

5. Have the children read or listen to the expository piece to find out more about the topic.

6. After the reading/listening, tell the children they will have 3 minutes to add to their list.

COWS

Before

Cows are animals. They lived on farms. They eat grass and hay. They have babies called calves.

4 ideas

After

Cows have two stomachs. They chew their cuds. They never eat meat. Black and white cows are called Holsteins, and they give the most milk. Daddy cows are called bulls.

6 ideas

7. When the time is up, ask the children to label the first part of the list "before" and the second part "after" (see illustration).

8. For a greater challenge: Ask the children to write two short paragraphs about cows, using the ideas from both lists. Give them lined paper with sentence stems for each paragraph. Tell them that this time they will create complete sentences from the ideas on their lists and self-edit for spelling and correct punctuation.

ASSESSMENT   Evaluate the children's writing based upon the difference in quantity of ideas in the first and second lists. Were the children able to augment their lists after reading (hearing) the story? Were the children able to correctly identify details in the story?

Notes for next time . . .

_____

_____

_____

_____

_____

_____

_____

_____

_____

_____

_____

Picture Paragraphs

**SUGGESTED
GRADE LEVEL** *2–3*

PURPOSE   One of the most difficult skills to teach children is how to turn groups of sentences into a cohesive paragraph. This activity demonstrates to children how they can read their own work and, using their own drawings, determine which sentences go with which key concepts.

MATERIALS
- A writing draft from each child
- Colored pencils
- Drawing paper
- Scissors
- Paste
- Sturdy cardboard

PROCEDURE

1. Ask the children each to procure a draft of a story on which they are currently working.

2. Invite the children to make a series of rough sketches that tell about each of the events in the story.

3. Ask the children to reread their piece to decide which sentences could go together and tell about the first picture.

4. When they have selected the sentences, have them draw a circle around each sentence that might go with that picture, using the same colored pencil.

5. Have them repeat these steps for each of their drawings, using a different colored pencil for each of the pictures.

6. Explain that each group of sentences that accompanies a drawing is called a paragraph, a group of sentences that all are about the same topic.

7. Provide scissors, paste, and sturdy cardboard so the children can rearrange their sentences and paragraphs by cutting and pasting as they find a more logical sequence for them.

The Dog's Adventure

Once there was a little dog that wandered off into the dark forest. He didn't know where he was going. He didn't know where his home was.

Soon the dog came upon a little man who seemed kind. The dog asked, "Mister, do you know where I live?" The man answered, "No, I sure don't."

Then the man reached down and picked up the dog. The dog trusted him. But guess what? The man took the dog right to the pound!

ASSESSMENT   Assess the children's ability to determine the main ideas in stories by the pictures they draw. Assess their ability to determine supporting details by the sentences they select to go with these pictures, as well as the topic sentences they choose. Observe them as they reorder the sentences and pictures to determine if they are able to detect the sequence in the story.

Notes for next time . . .

_____

_____

Five Senses

SUGGESTED
GRADE LEVEL   *1–2*

PURPOSE   This activity provides the visual stimulation to allow learners, especially ELL, to think about words to complete sentence stems that tell how a balloon looks, feels, tastes, smells, and sounds.

MATERIALS
- Enough balloons for each group of five children
- String to tie the balloons
- Sentence stems for each of the five senses (see illustration)
- Overhead projector and blank transparency

PROCEDURE

1. Place children into groups of five. Give each group one balloon and help them blow up their balloons and tie the ends.

2. Give each group five sheets of paper. On each sheet of paper is written a sentence stem for one of the five senses. Read each of the sentence stems with the children.

3. Begin with the sense of sight. Ask each child to take turns holding the balloon and thinking of words that tell about how it looks. Assign one child from the group to that sense and determine which word(s) will be used to complete the sentence stem.

4. Using the overhead projector, demonstrate how the children are to write the word(s) to complete the sentence.

5. Go to the next sense, hearing. Ask the children to pass the balloon around in their group and brainstorm words that tell how the balloon sounds. Assign a different child within the group to decide which word(s) or phrases to use and finish the sentence.

6. Repeat this procedure until the balloon has been considered using all the five senses.

7. Have each group share its ideas with the rest of the class.

8. Make class books about balloons and the five senses, encouraging each child to illustrate his or her contribution.

4 *Five Senses*

Continued.

My Balloon

My balloon looks like _a blue pickle._

My balloon sounds like _a squeaky old door._

My balloon smells like _a new baby doll._

My balloon feels like _a smooth stone._

My balloon tastes like _yucky bubble gum._

ASSESSMENT   Use a clipboard to observe the contributions of each child in each group. Note whether each child understands the concept of each sense and if each is able to think of appropriate words to describe that sense. Finally, invite each child to read his or her group's contributions to you, asking the child to track while reading the new words and the sentence stems.

Notes for next time . . .

_____

_____

_____

What Do Writers Do?

SUGGESTED GRADE LEVEL *K–3*

PURPOSE This is an activity to help young children understand the writing process and to give the teacher some insight into how students think about writing and what it entails.

MATERIALS ● Chart paper

PROCEDURE

1. After reading an enjoyable piece of children's literature to the children, spend some time discussing the author. Personalize this person by telling children where he or she is from, summarize the plots of other books he or she has written, and provide any other interesting biographical details you have researched. Optional: Invite a local author to talk to children.

2. Have the children brainstorm all the things they think the author had to do to write the book. Ask them specifically: What do good writers do?

3. On the chart paper, write all the ideas the children offer, discussing them one at a time.

4. Leave the chart in a prominent place in the classroom so the children can refer to it when they are writing. Review the ideas on the chart before the children are to be engaged in creative writing assignments.

5. Encourage the children to add new ideas to the chart as they think of them.

What Do Good Writers Do?

Writers think of ideas.

They make you interested in what they have to say.

They plan their story for an audience.

Good writers get suggestions from somebody.

They try to write so others can read what they wrote.

Authors have a beginning, a middle part, and an ending.

They use lots of juicy words.

Good writers use complete sentences.

They make you feel happy or sad because of their writing.

ASSESSMENT

With this activity, you can clearly see if children are beginning to see themselves as writers and understand the tasks involved in writing. Use this activity primarily to give you perspective on the direction your writing instruction has to take to promote awareness of the various facets of the writing process. Use the activity several times during the year to measure children's progress in understanding the writing process.

Notes for next time . . .

_____

_____

_____

_____

_____

_____

_____

_____

_____

_____

_____

_____

_____

_____

_____

_____

_____

_____

Descriptive Recodes

SUGGESTED GRADE LEVEL *2–3*

PURPOSE
This is an enjoyable way to allow children to take the basic writing of decodable texts and make it more descriptive and interesting through the use of enhanced vocabulary and more sophisticated phrasing.

MATERIALS
- Decodable text at children's independent reading level
- Paper
- Writing utensils
- Overhead projector
- Overhead transparency of a page from decodable text

PROCEDURE

1. Select a page at random from a decodable text, project it on the overhead projector and read it with the children.

2. Model aloud how you would revise several paragraphs from the text, making it more descriptive and interesting by adding juicy words to replace the tired ones and by adding dialogue, emotions, phrases, and other details to make the writing more vibrant.

3. After you have modeled several paragraphs, elicit suggestions for revising from the children.

4. Read the new page of text and compare it with the original. Solicit opinions as to which is more interesting. Why?

5. Assign a page (a sentence for emerging writers) of decodable text to pairs of students. Ask each pair to rewrite their page (sentence), adding descriptive phrases, juicy words, and other more interesting details.

6. When each group has finished, ask the children to practice reading their revised page (sentence) of text.

> **Nat was Sad**
>
> Nat sat on the mat. Nat was sad.
>
> A rat sat on the mat. The rat was sad.
>
> A fat cat sat on the mat.
>
> Was the cat sad? The cat was not sad.
>
> The cat ate the rat. Nat saw that the cat ate the rat. Nat was sad!

7. Invite one child from each pair to read their new page (sentence) to the whole group, in order.

8. Discuss how the additions made the text more interesting, and why.

ASSESSMENT   As pairs of children are working on this lesson, observe and take anecdotal notes of each child's participation. Afterward, have individual children tell you a juicy word they remember that made the story more interesting and have them tell why. During subsequent individual writing time and conferencing with the children, check to see if they are incorporating more description in their writing.

Notes for next time . . .

_____

_____

_____

_____

_____

_____

_____

_____

_____

_____

_____

_____

Provocative Paintings

SUGGESTED GRADE LEVEL *2–3*

PURPOSE

Fine art can be a delightful stimulus to writing if children are asked provocative questions and are allowed to respond in their own words about their reactions. This activity shows how to integrate art with writing to create a rich blend of the two.

MATERIALS

- Reprints of fine art paintings (suggestions: Monet, Cassatt, O'Keefe, Picasso)
- A notepad for each child

PROCEDURE

1. Introduce a fine art painting to the children, telling a bit about the artist, his or her life and times, and the title of the piece.

2. Do the same with five paintings over several days.

3. When all the paintings have been introduced, hang them, gallery-style, in a prominent place in the room.

4. Tell the children they are to become "art critics" and will write down their reactions to their favorite painting. Write a list of questions on the board and read each one with the children.

5. Invite the children to walk around and study the paintings. Ask them to select their favorite, and jot down some words and phrases about their selection in response to the following questions:

   Which painting speaks to you most? Why?

   What would you name this painting?

   What in your life does the painting remind you of?

> **Contrast Frame**
>
> Water Lilies and Hand with Flowers are different in a few ways. First, <u>Water Lilies doesn't have people and Hand with Flowers has two people's hands in it.</u> Second, <u>Water Lilies has soft colors in it while Hand with Flowers has bright colors in it.</u> But the way the paintings are most different is that <u>Water Lilies looks real while Hand with Flowers looks like a cartoon.</u>

What are some people, places, or things the painting makes you think of?

What would you do differently if you had painted this picture?

Write down some words or phrases that you think of when you see this painting.

6. When the children have finished jotting down their thoughts, have them choose a partner who has selected a painting different from theirs.

7. Have them use a Contrast Frame to compare the two paintings (see illustration) using their lists of words and phrases.

8. Encourage pairs of students to read their Contrast Frames to the rest of the class, with one child reading while the other points to the appropriate painting.

ASSESSMENT   The Contrast Frame provides a scaffold that enables children with even rudimentary writing abilities to compose a paragraph. Evaluate paragraphs on the basis of complete thoughts and contrasting ideas, while adjusting expectations of complexity to each child's developmental stage.

Notes for next time . . .

_____

_____

_____

_____

_____

_____

Triangular Triplets

(Adapted from Cecil, For the Love of Language, *1994)*

8

SUGGESTED GRADE LEVEL   *2–3*

PURPOSE   In this motivational introduction to writing poetry, children practice rhyming while creating simple three-line poems.

MATERIALS
- One sheet of plain white paper for each child
- One sheet of colored construction paper for each child
- Scissors
- Paste
- Scrap paper
- Pencils

PROCEDURE

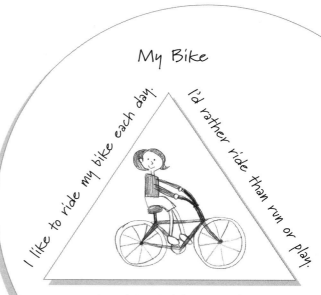

My Bike

I like to ride my bike each day.

I'd rather ride than run or play.

I meet a lot of friends this way!

1. Distribute colored construction paper and a sheet of plain white paper to each child.

2. Ask the children to draw a picture of themselves in the center of the white paper, engaged in their favorite activity.

3. Demonstrate how to draw a triangle around their drawing, cut it out, and paste it near the top of their construction paper.

4. Read the sample poem to the children (see illustration). Discuss how the ending words all rhyme and how each line tells something about the activity in the triangle.

5. Guide them to use the picture in their triangle as inspiration for a three-lined rhymed poem.

6. Have them write drafts of their poem on the scrap paper while you offer suggestions for easy rhyming words.

8 Triangular Triplets

Continued.

7. When they finish their poems, have them write one line on each side of the triangle to form a "running commentary" about the activity occurring inside the triangle.

ASSESSMENT Check to see that poems have (1) three lines, (2) three words that rhyme at the end of each line, and (3) each line corresponding to the picture.

Notes for next time . . .

Mind Pictures

SUGGESTED
GRADE LEVEL *K–3*

PURPOSE   To provide children with a wealth of ideas that always will be at their disposal as they write independently, children's mind pictures can serve as the bridge between pictorial imagination and oral language, igniting written language.

MATERIALS
- Construction paper folded into four sections
- Writing paper
- Crayons
- Tape recorder for each child (optional)

PROCEDURE

1. Gather the children around you on the floor in a relaxed fashion.

2. Tell the children to close their eyes and make their mind as empty as possible.

3. Say: Now I want you to keep your mind empty for as long as you can. As soon as a picture comes into your mind, raise your hand. Wait until all hands are up, then discuss various mind pictures.

4. Say: I am now going to ask you to put your last picture back into your mind and hold it there as long as you can. When that picture changes to a new picture, raise your hand. Again, allow the children to share their new images.

5. When the children are quite proficient at creating pictures in their mind, offer them a "cliffhanger" to complete with their mind pictures (see examples).

6. Distribute paper and crayons. Ask the children to consult their mind pictures to determine what happens next in the story. Have the children draw pictures, in the sections created by the folds, of the events as they occur in sequence. Encourage them to return to their mind pictures when they think they are unsure of what happens next.

7. As an optional intermediary step for younger children, allow them to discuss their drawings with a partner or tell the story prompted by their drawings into a tape recorder.

8. Distribute writing paper. Invite the children to put their sequential drawings into written form. Later, invite the children to share their stories with the rest of the class.

Continued.

- You are entering a room in an attic. It is raining and you can hear the soft patter of raindrops. You wander around the attic and notice an old rocking horse and a stuffed rabbit with an ear missing. You walk toward a broken window and see a large spider web. You notice a large mirror on the far wall of the attic. It has fancy gold decorations and lots of dust. When you start to brush it off, you discover, to your surprise, that you can walk right through it. You push your body through the mirror and suddenly you see . . .

- You are exploring a deep, dark cave. Suddenly you hear a loud, booming voice. You try to find your way back to the entrance, but all the rooms in the cave look alike. You panic as you realize that the voice is coming closer and closer. You turn around and finally see who it is . . .

- You are skin-diving off the coast of Australia. You are having fun playing hide-and-seek with the dolphins and friendly parrot fish. Suddenly you spy an old abandoned ship and you dive down to examine it more closely. You open the door to the captain's quarters and you are amazed to find . . .

ASSESSMENT   Depending on their developmental stage, have the children participate in this activity by drawing, by orally sharing, or by writing. In any case, look for vivid imagery and the development of a sequential story with a beginning, middle, and end. Have the children read or tell you their story while you check for these features.

Notes for next time . . .

_____

_____

_____

Add-On Stories

10

SUGGESTED GRADE LEVEL *2–3*

PURPOSE With this unique writing activity, children can participate in creating a narrative piece regardless of their level of writing proficiency. Narrative structure is reinforced, and the children see, graphically, that many plots are possible from a single beginning sentence.

MATERIALS
- Writing paper
- Writing utensils
- Story Starters (see illustration)

PROCEDURE

1. Group children into three each and distribute writing materials. Explain that each group will be writing a part of shared stories.

2. Write a story starter on the board and read it to the children. Ask them to copy it on the top of their papers.

3. Tell the children they will now have 10 minutes to begin a story using the lead-in sentence they have just written on their papers. When the 10 minutes are up, ask them to finish the sentence they are writing and pass their paper to the person sitting to their left in the group and receive the paper of the child to their right. *Note:* You will need to "float" around to read writing that appears illegible to fledgling readers.

4. Explain that they will read now the story beginning from the person on their right and then add a middle part.

5. When 10 minutes have passed, ask them again to pass their paper to the person sitting to their left and receive the paper from the child on their right. This time they will read the paper be-

Sample Story Starters

The puppy was looking in at the warm fire and whimpering.

I opened the front door and there was a large box sitting on the doorstep.

I was shocked when I noticed my hands were growing large and hairy.

There he was on my desk, the tiniest little pony you ever saw.

My friends said the old house was haunted and I just had to find out.

"Three wishes," said the wise lady, "and use them with care."

10 *Add-On Stories*
Continued.

fore them and create an original story ending for it. Explain that sometimes a person will have written no more than a sentence and that is okay; the idea is to keep to the idea started by the previous writer.

6. When the story endings have been completed, collect them and read them to the class, remarking on the diversity of stories made possible by one lead-in sentence! Return the stories to the groups for group editing, illustrations, and incorporation into a class book.

ASSESSMENT   As you are helping struggling writers with this activity, check to see if they are able to create story beginnings, middles, and endings. Further, ask group members to identify the beginning, middle, and end of their shared stories.

Notes for next time . . .

_____

_____

_____

_____

_____

_____

_____

_____

_____

_____

_____

_____

Other Ideas & Activities

LISTS

Encourage the children, in small share groups, to list five ideas on a topic, such as: Five Things To Do Last, Five Things Not to Say to a Shark, or Five Things We Don't Like to Do.

WHAT HAPPENS NEXT?

Read a short story to the children and stop at the most exciting point. Discuss with the children what they think might happen next. Ask the children to write an ending using one of the brainstormed ideas or another idea of their own choosing.

PEN PALS

Find another class of students in a neighboring school or in another city or state. Introduce friendly letter writing by having your students initiate correspondence with the students there by telling about themselves. Provide a template letter for emergent writers.

CLASSIFIEDS

After reading the children some advertisements from the classified advertising section of a newspaper, ask them to think how they might sell themselves. Have them create a small classified ad for selling themselves by listing their most positive features and qualities.

MAIL SERVICE

Put a mailbox in your classroom where children can write messages to you or to each other (only "good" and "true" messages). Utilize the "service" to tell children when they have behaved well.

I AM . . .

Have the children draw pictures of themselves, including any physical characteristic they think makes them different from others. Ask them to finish the sentence: I am . . . at least five times at the bottom of the drawing. Provide a time when children can share their drawings and "I am . . ." statements.

PICTURE PERFECT

Take pictures of each child in the class and hang them around the room. Invite other classmates to write "good and true" comments about other children on paper positioned under each picture. You can contribute, too!

SLOGAN STATEMENTS

Have the children keep a list of slogans they notice on people's tee-shirts and on bumper stickers. Discuss these and what they say about the person who has them. Encourage the children to each write a personal slogan telling something about themselves.

- **SILLY EVENT**

  Ask the children to write an invitation to a humorous, fictitious event, such as a crocodile hunt, a tiddly winks contest, an animal marriage, and so on.

- **PICTO-BIOGRAPHY**

  Ask the children to bring in old and recent pictures of themselves, their family, their pets, friends, and so forth. Give them long sheets of paper on which to paste the pictures. For each picture, have them write one sentence telling about the part of their life shown in that picture.

- **HAND-OUT**

  Have the children trace their hand on a piece of paper. On the outline of their hand, ask them to write all the things they can do with their hands.

- **PLAYGROUND WATCH**

  Ask the children to watch a person they don't know on the playground for 10 minutes. Then have them write what they think the person was thinking. Extra challenge: Have them hypothesize a name for the person and describe the person's daily routine.

- **SALESPERSON**

  Select as many items from the classified ads as there are children in your class. Allow each child to select an item and, using descriptive language and an illustration, create a poster convincing others to buy it.

- **PROVOCATIVE QUESTIONS**

  Use provocative questions, such as "What if animals could talk?" or "What if everyone looked exactly alike?" to generate a discussion. Then make a list of advantages and disadvantages to such an event occurring. Finally, have children write a brief paragraph stating their personal opinion about the topic.

Children's Literature List

Anholt, Catherine, and Anholt, Laurence. *All About You.* (New York: Viking, 1991).

A series of questions asking children to tell about themselves. Possible illustrated answers are included. Provides preparation for writing an autobiographical piece.

Asch, Frank. *Ziggy Piggy and the Three Little Pigs.* (New York: Kids Can, 1998).

A take-off on a familiar story. Ted, Frank, and Ned warn their brother Ziggy about the Big Bad Wolf. They tell him he should build a house to keep himself safe but Ziggy builds a raft instead. He saves the day for his brothers. Children can create similar take-offs on other familiar fairy tales.

McDonnell, Flora. *I Love Animals.* (New York: Candlewick, 1994).

Drawing and words showing why a little girl loves all animals. Repeated lines provide opportunities for choral or shared reading. Structure provides an ideal model for writing.

Numeroff, Laura, illustrated by Felicia Bond. *If You Give a Pig a Pancake.* (New York: Geringer/HarperCollins, 1998).

A circular tale that takes the reader/listener through a day in the life of a girl and her pig that happens to love pancakes. Using this scaffold with another animal and object (e.g., "If you give a dog a bone . . ."), children can be invited to write their own circular tale.

Simon, Semour, illustrated with photos. *Autumn Across America.* (New York: Hyperion, 1993).

Seasonal changes from east to west across America captured in striking photographs. Simon points out how animals and plants also change with the seasons. The photos can be used as provocative writing prompts.

Other Resources for Teaching Writing

Children's Writing: Perspectives from Research, by Karin L. Dahl and Nancy Farnan (Newark, DE: International Reading Association, 1998).

Explores the beliefs teachers have shared about classroom practices and children's writing processes. The authors highlight representative research studies, describing them with a focus on classroom application. Timely topics such as writing workshops and writing and technology are included.

Classrooms That Work: They Can All Read and Write, 2d edition, by Patricia M. Cunningham and Richard L. Allington (New York: Longman, 1999).

A plethora of ideas for developing readers, writers, and thinkers using a variety of authentic narrative and expository texts. The authors share the viewpoint that phonics instruction is necessary, but it is not enough to create joyful readers who construct their own meaning from text.

For the Love of Language: Poetry Scaffolds for Every Learner, by Nancy Lee Cecil (Winnipeg, Manitoba: Peguis Publishers, 1994).

Ideas to help children explore many types of poetry. Each poetry activity includes a description, an easy-to-follow pattern, and a lead-in activity to help motivate children and help the teacher prepare for the session. Also includes samples of poetry written by children.

Fresh Takes on Using Journals to Teach Beginning Writers: Five-Minute Mini-Lessons, Skill-Building Strategies, and Irresistible Activities That Inspire Children to Write, by Jim Henry (Jefferson City, MO: Scholastic Professional Books, 1999).

A model of journal writing that helps beginning writers become engaged, proficient authors of poetry, fiction, and prose. Journal writing becomes dynamic through sharing, demonstration lessons, and independent writing time.

Getting the Most Out of Morning Message and Other Shared Writing Lessons, by Carleen daCruz and Mary Browning Schulman (Jefferson City, MO: Scholastic Professional Books, 1999).

Photos, samples of student work, classroom dialogues, and lesson plans to illustrate innovative techniques for teaching beginning writers by writing with them. Also includes tips on creating hands-on literacy resources such as Word Walls, Big Books, and slide shows.

Know and Tell: A Writing Pedagogy of Disclosure, Genre, and Membership, by David Bleich (Portsmouth, NH: Heinemann, 1998).

Intended for English teachers, but adaptations of concepts can be made for much younger students. The author stresses that all writing must be viewed in the context of the immediate social scene, the writer's interests and feelings.

Reading-Writing Connections: From Theory to Practice, 3d edition, by Mary F. Heller (New York: Longman, 2000).

An opportunity to look inside the classroom and see how theory and research can be transformed into practical, developmentally appropriate literacy instruction. The text offers effective teaching of the reading-writing connection through direct instruction and child-centered activity, encouraging children to become lifelong readers and writers.

25 Mini-Lessons for Teaching Writing, by Adele Fiderer (Jefferson City, MO: Scholastic Professional Books, 1999).

A wealth of samples of children's writing so students can see good writing by peers. The lessons focus on writing skill elements such as choosing pertinent topics, organizing ideas, writing clearly, and learning how to edit.

In Closing

1. After using the activities in this section, what insights have you gained about how children learn to use the writing process? What did you also discover about yourself as a teacher of writing by teaching these activities?

2. Which of the activities did you think were particularly effective for reinforcing the following components of the writing process? Why?

   - Prewriting

   - Drafting

   - Sharing

   - Revising

   - Editing

   - Publishing

3. Which of the activities did you think was the most effective for developing the following literacy goals? Why?

   - Awareness that writing is constructing meaning

   - A positive attitude toward writing and its conventions

   - An appreciation of self as writer

   - Development of self as editor and collaborator

   - Interest in experimenting with writing in a variety of formats

4. What did you discover about children's need to choose a topic of interest to them so as to become fully engaged in the writing process? Which activity best underscored this need?

5. Select an activity that offered you the most insight into the writing abilities of your learners. What did you discover? Cite examples of specific children with whom you worked.

6. Several of the activities asked you to provide the children with scaffolds or templates to help them to begin writing on a certain topic. What might be the advantages and disadvantages of using these devices? How might using such a device allow children to achieve more than they might without that device?

7. Certain activities had children use their senses before they began writing. How was writing encouraged as a result of these activities? Give examples of specific children and how they responded as a result of the activities.

8. Some activities began with oral discussion or brainstorming. How do you think these precursors to writing provided children with ideas? Give examples of specific children and how they were engaged in writing as a result.

9. Which activities were most difficult for your ELL children? What did you observe about their difficulties? How could you revise these activities to make them more accessible for your ELL children?

10. Identify a child you think has highly developed writing ability. What are the characteristics of the child? Did his or her behavior during the activities differ from that of the other children? Describe and explain the differences, if any.

VIDEO SELF-ASSESSMENT

(With permission from Linda Current)

Making a video of a lesson you teach to a class is an outstanding way for you to gain heightened awareness of what you do well and in what areas you may need improvement. Be aware that the first few times you view the tape, you may find yourself focusing on the superficial—your "bad hair day," your clothes, or the pounds you wish you could lose. This is normal and to be expected but, of course, not the purpose for the taping.

After viewing the tape in a general way a few times, play it again, this time focusing more intently on the specific behaviors listed below. You might have to view the tape separately for each behavior, because it is difficult to concentrate on everything you are doing in one viewing.

Video Self-Assessment

In the spaces below, write down any observations, insights, or feelings you have about your lesson and your teaching behaviors. Particularly be on the lookout for any behavior patterns.

Note: Optionally, a friend or colleague may observe your teaching and respond to the following questions. This could replace your video self-assessment or serve as additional feedback.

1. How does my voice sound? Pitch? Volume? Expression? Pace?

_____

_____

_____

_____

2. How does my face and body language convey my enthusiasm for the lesson? Do I smile? Do I make eye contact with the children?

_____

_____

_____

_____

3. Do I move around the room appropriately as I teach? Do I make nonverbal connections with children during the lesson?

_____

_____

_____

_____

4. Do I reflect "with-it-ness?" Do I project awareness of what is happening in all parts of the classroom with all the children? Do some children glance up at me to determine if I am "with-it" or not?

_____

_____

_____

_____

A Video Self-Assessment

Continued.

5. What is the approximate ratio of teacher talk compared to student talk?

_____

_____

_____

_____

6. Are the children on-task? Who is not? Do I notice? What do I do about it?

_____

_____

_____

_____

7. Is the noise level appropriate for the lesson? Do I set noise level expectations in advance?

_____

_____

_____

_____

8. Do I lead into the lesson in a stimulating way? Do I set a purpose for the lesson?

_____

_____

_____

_____

9. Am I aware of how my second language learners are able to access the lesson? What specific provisions do I make to add comprehensible input into the lesson?

_____

_____

_____

_____

Continued.

10. Do I appear to have a clear objective for my teaching? Do I reach my objective? How?

_____

_____

_____

_____

11. Do my procedures follow a logical sequence?

_____

_____

_____

_____

12. Do I give the children clear instructions and check that they understand what they are to do?

_____

_____

_____

_____

13. How do I use praise? Count the number of instances of positive reinforcement and the instances of negative reinforcement. What are my interpretations of these numbers?

_____

_____

_____

_____

14. On what area of classroom management do I need to focus?

_____

_____

_____

_____

Video Self-Assessment

Continued.

15. What are the strengths of the lesson?

_____

_____

_____

_____

14. What are the strengths of my teaching performance?

_____

_____

_____

_____

16. What are the problems, if any, with the lesson?

_____

_____

_____

_____

17. What would I change in the lesson next time?

_____

_____

_____

_____

18. What would I change in my teaching performance next time?

_____

_____

_____

_____

Notes and other observations:

INSTRUCTION AND REFLECTION PROFILE

This profile contains two separate parts. The first part comprises the reflection a teacher must do when planning a lesson, before actually teaching it. Teachers must make the following decisions when planning a lesson:

What outcomes are to be achieved?

What grouping configuration shall I use?

What methods are most appropriate?

Which activities will best help me meet my goals?

What materials will be most beneficial?

How will I determine whether children have met my objectives?

The first part of the profile is to be completed before you do your lesson to help you consider each of these important questions.

Instruction and Reflection Profile

Continued.

The second part of the profile is to be completed after you have completed your lesson. Teachers continually learn about the effectiveness of their lessons and the effectiveness of their own teaching performance by the reflecting they do after each lesson. During this second reflection, they revisit the decisions they made to design their lesson and determine, by considering the same questions, if they have met their instructional goals.

Complete Part I before you teach your lesson. Complete Part II after your lesson.

Part I

GOALS

What are your goals for student learning for this lesson? Why have you chosen these goals? How do you expect the students to behave differently as a result of your teaching?

_____

_____

_____

_____

_____

GROUPING

How will you group your students for instruction? Why?

_____

_____

_____

_____

METHODS

What teaching method(s) will you use for this lesson?

_____

_____

_____

_____

_____

B Instruction and Reflection Profile
Continued.

ACTIVITIES

List the activities you have planned and the time you have allocated for each.

_____

_____

_____

_____

_____

MATERIALS

What instructional materials will you use? Why have you chosen these materials?

_____

_____

_____

_____

ASSESSMENT

How and when do you plan to assess student learning on the content of this lesson? Why have you chosen this form of assessment?

_____

_____

_____

_____

B Instruction and Reflection Profile

Continued.

Part II

GOALS

Did all the children achieve the learning goals you had set for them? How do you know that?

_____

_____

_____

_____

_____

_____

GROUPING

How would you group your students for this lesson in the future? Why?

_____

_____

_____

_____

_____

_____

METHODS

In what ways were your teaching methods effective? Why do you think so?

_____

_____

_____

_____

_____

_____

Instruction and Reflection Profile

Continued.

ACTIVITIES

In what ways did your activities help you to meet your goals? Might you use other activities instead in the future? Why?

_____

_____

_____

_____

_____

_____

MATERIALS

In what ways were your materials effective/ineffective? Why do you think so?

_____

_____

_____

_____

_____

_____

ASSESSMENT

Did anything occur during this lesson to change your assessment plan? If so, how has it changed? How will your assessment inform future instruction?

_____

_____

_____

_____

_____

_____

LESSON PLAN FORMAT

Teaching often is considered both an art and a science. The "art" element in teaching is the special magic teachers bring to the classroom through the force of their personality, creativity, and caring for the children, as well as the personal way they orchestrate the activities that take place in the classroom.

The "science" element of teaching is in the reflection that occurs while designing lessons to be motivational and to meet the developmental needs of all learners, and also while considering the strengths and weaknesses of the lesson after it has been taught.

Lesson Plan Format

Continued.

This instrument may be used as is, or with modifications, to help you design an effective literacy lesson for young children. Space for self-reflection is included at the end. Use the space provided or use additional paper to complete your self-evaluation.

1. **PURPOSE OF THE LESSON**

    Why have I chosen to teach this lesson?

    _____

    _____

    _____

    _____

    _____

2. **BEHAVIORAL OBJECTIVES**

    What will children be able to do/do better as a result of this lesson?

    _____

    _____

    _____

    _____

    _____

3. **MOTIVATION**

    What will I do/say to get the children engaged in what I want them to do?

    _____

    _____

    _____

    _____

    _____

Lesson Plan Format

Continued.

4. PROCEDURES

Lesson development: What steps will I use to develop this lesson in an organized fashion?

_____

_____

_____

_____

_____

5. ASSESSMENT

Evaluation of the lesson: How will I know that children have met my objectives for the lesson? What exactly to I expect them to be able to do/do better as a result of my lesson?

_____

_____

_____

_____

_____

6. SELF-EVALUATION OF LESSON

How do I think the lesson went? What happened that I did not expect? What worked well? What did _not_ work well? What would I do differently? How has my assessment informed future instruction?

_____

_____

_____

_____

_____

_____